LOVE THE BODY
YOU WERE BORN WITH

LOVE THE BODY YOU WERE BORN WITH

A Ten-Step Workbook for Women

Monica Dixon, M.S., R.D.

A Perigee Book

This book is a fully revised edition of
*Love the Body You Were Born With: 12 Steps
to a Healthier, Happier You*, originally
published in 1994 by Monica Dixon.

A Perigee Book
Published by The Berkley Publishing Group
200 Madison Avenue
New York, NY 10016

First edition: January 1996

Published simultaneously in Canada.

Library of Congress Cataloging-in-Publication Data

Dixon, Monica A.
Love the body you were born with : a ten-step workbook for women /
Monica A. Dixon.—1st ed.
p.   cm.
"A Perigee book."
Includes bibliographical references.
ISBN 0-399-51975-0
1. Body image.   2. Women—Psychology.   3. Leanness—Psychological
aspects.   4. Sex (Psychology)   I. Title.
BF697.5.B63D58   1996
155.6'33—dc20   95-33252
CIP

Printed in the United States of America

10 9 8 7 6 5 4 3 2 1

For my brother Conrad—
Because your life was far too short

Contents

Your body is where you'll be spending the rest of your life . . . Isn't it time you made it your home?

Acknowledgments

I owe a debt of deep gratitude to the thousands of women throughout the last ten years who have honored me by sharing their stories and opening their hearts to me. These women shared deeply personal views of what it means to be a woman in today's society, and their sometimes overwhelming feelings of confusion and guilt surrounding their bodies and food planted the early seeds for this book. Their stories of anger, fear, frustration, and lifestyle changes touched my own life. As I bore witness to their stories, I came to find a new voice of my own prompting changes in my life as a woman and kindling my passion for writing about their experiences.

I would also like to acknowledge the tremendous assistance of Dr. Nancy Keim, Dr. Herman Johnson, and Dr. Marta Van Loan at the United States Department of Agriculture's Western Nutrition Human Research Center in San Francisco. I deeply appreciate their invitation to work with their weight loss and exercise research study participants to explore my ideas about the relationships of eating and psychology. I not only learned invaluable lessons from the research participants, but much from the research team as well about the role of the scientist in nutrition and exercise research.

The support of my family and friends has been unwavering throughout this writing process. To my grandmother, Monica Biermeier, who was thirty years ahead of her time in understanding the importance of good nutrition in raising children, I will never forget the cod liver oil every evening. Thanks to my mother, Katharine Ciokiewicz, who somehow, even in the craziest of times growing up, fed us the most healthy, nourishing meals, sometimes seemingly out of nowhere. She taught me early on that eating well was vitally important for accomplishing what I wanted out of life. And a heartfelt thank-you to my brother Daryl, who for thirty-five years has always managed to make me laugh and believed in me, even in the worst of times. To Don and Mary Beth, thank you for listening eternally to my often half-baked ideas. There are no better gifts in life than friends like you. Thank you to Gloria Gritz, a brilliant writer and friend who patiently polished the first crude drafts and believed from the beginning that all women should be able to read my message. And to her son, Richard Gritz, an incredibly talented computer whiz, thank you for the many late nights teaching me Macintoshes could be much more than word processors.

Last, and most importantly, I would like to acknowledge and affirm my husband, Rod, for his never-ending support over the last eighteen years of my life. His support of my dreams has been unyielding, and he has fostered and encouraged every step of the way my growth and transformations as a woman. He has taught me the invaluable importance of being able to laugh at one's self, that dads can be great "moms" while I travel with my message, and that a good night's sleep never hurt anyone.

Preface

The hours immediately following my workshops on body image, eating, and sexuality are always the most difficult but immensely rewarding for me professionally. It seems I am furtively pursued by women, from dark corners, behind staircases or the bushes outside. Through teary eyes, they share their unique and poignant stories of endless dieting, shame with their bodies and sexuality, or past histories of abuse to their bodies by themselves or others. Others shed tears, not so much for themselves, but for their daughters they love so dearly as they watch them physically and verbally abuse their bodies with self-hatred. For many of these women, they say this is the first time these deep emotional issues have been validated for them and discussed and brought into the open. Their greatest gain has been learning other women suffer with the same deep hatred of their bodies as they do. These moments in conversation serve to enrage me at the incredible loss of valuable life experiences spent hating the only body we are given, and refuel my passion to continue my work.

Yet of equal interest are the comments made to me by men in my audiences: "I never knew this was such a problem for women" or "Thank you, thank you, I now understand a bit more why my wife is so cruel on herself." These men, the other half of many of our relationships, seem deeply confused and concerned over the harshness the women they love experience toward their bodies. These men aren't the ones making large amounts of money off the latest dieting fad for women or perpetuating the advertisements that victimize women, but men who truly love the woman standing in front of the mirror calling herself an "elephant." It is time that we recognize that learning to love our bodies and revel in their uniqueness is not just a woman's issue; it is often the plight of the men who love us as well.

I would encourage you to journey the pages of this book with other women who you may feel safe and comfortable with. I continue to receive calls from women throughout the country who have gathered five or ten friends together to work through and discuss one chapter at a time. The women report a sense of freedom and strength gathered from hearing others share stories similar to their own. My mother's generation had the "coffee klatch" to share with each other and provide community, while consequent generations have tended to become more isolated from others through time and career demands. Perhaps in some ways this isolation from other women has heightened our feelings of anxiety and disgust at our bodies and left us feeling the "lone ranger."

I must voice a word of caution though, should you decide to meet in groups. Some of the issues in this book that may surface can be very painful for some women if not resolved without professional help. I strongly encourage you to seek the assistance of a professional therapist or counselor well versed in women's issues, should this occur.

Finally, I cannot encourage you enough to live this book and make it your own. Write in it, do each exercise and note in the margins your thoughts. Each step that you take on paper will bring you that much closer to truly loving the body you were born with. I wish for you a journey of both growth and freedom.

LOVE THE BODY
YOU WERE BORN WITH

Who Could Love *This* Body?

All I want out of life are world peace and thin thighs.
Actually, I don't care that much about world peace.

As American women, we've been programmed to hate our bodies.

That coffee-mug inscription cuts through the hype and gets to the heart of one of the biggest obstacles to self-fulfillment facing American women today. From the time we were little girls, we have been programmed to hate our bodies. We've bought Madison Avenue's vision of the ideal woman and let ourselves be duped into believing that starvation diets and marathon workout sessions would give us Barbie-doll thighs.

The fact that 98 percent of us cannot achieve those results under *any* circumstances doesn't much matter. We feel like failures. We hate our thighs. We hate our stomachs. We hate our upper arms. In short, we hate our bodies. So we keep trying to change them.

The result? Most of us have developed an incredibly complicated relationship with food.

One in four of us is obese, but we're obsessed with dieting and slimness.

As a group, we range from being preoccupied to being obsessed with dieting and slimness. Incredibly, this has happened in an era when fattening fast food is served to 20 percent of Americans on any given day and the dessert industry is flourishing. As we become heavier—one in four of us is obese—the advertising industry talks "lite."

It's no wonder huge numbers of women are starving themselves to death while even greater numbers are eating themselves into oblivion.

Eating disorders have skyrocketed in the last twenty years. Bulimia and anorexia nervosa have reached epidemic proportions among young women, while compulsive overeating is destroying the lives of countless others of all ages on the opposite end of the spectrum.

If you look at the continuum, you will see the bone-thin women suffering from anorexia nervosa on one end and the seriously obese on the other. Hundreds of books and articles have been written for and about these women at the extreme ends, and entire medical centers in some parts of the country are now devoted to helping them.

This workbook is designed for women in the middle of the continuum.

Anorexia   *Morbid*

Nervosa   *You* probably fall somewhere along the straight line.   *Obesity*

While their problems are heartbreaking and all too understandable to most of us, this workbook is designed for those who fit somewhere in the middle of the continuum. You may be ten or thirty or even fifty pounds over the weight the charts recommend, or you may not be overweight at all, simply believing some part of you, like those ubiquitous thighs, is obese. Perhaps, through the natural phases of a woman's life cycle—childbirth or menopause, for example—your body has changed, making you uncomfortable with the body you now own.

Not liking your body has high costs.

Not liking your body can extract a heavy toll. It's hard to take good care of something you don't like, much less respect. It's almost impossible to act beautiful and sexy when you feel fat and ugly. Relationships suffer. Sex lives suffer. Even your health can suffer.

Do you need help learning to love the body you were born with? In five minutes or less, you'll know the answer. Just take the quiz that follows. Don't stop to think about the questions—just go with your gut responses.

Do I Love *This* Body?

Check yes or no.

Yes   No

___ ___   1. I have struggled with my weight for years.

___ ___   2. I am very concerned about my weight.

___ ___   3. I am critical of my body.

___ ___   4. I tend to laugh off compliments about my appearance.

___ ___   5. I am very concerned about a body part or parts that I feel are either inadequate or *too* adequate.

___ ___   6. I am uncomfortable in social situations where I feel I'm being watched.

___ ___   7. I hate to wear a bathing suit in public.

___ ___   8. I am uncomfortable eating in public.

___ ___   9. I don't like my partner to see me naked.

___ ___   10. I don't like to see me naked.

___ ___   11. I feel ashamed of my body.

___ ___   12. I seek refuge under the sheets during lovemaking.

___ ___   13. I compare myself mentally to visual images of "ideal" women.

___ ___   14. I often tell myself I'll take control again in the morning and once again attempt to diet.

___ ___   15. I want to lose a prescribed amount of weight before I go on vacation or attend a wedding or fly home for my class reunion.

___ ___   16. When my partner says he loves me just the way I am, I wonder what the hell that's supposed to mean.

"Yes" on three or fewer:

Count your "yes" answers on the quiz. If you answered yes to fewer than three of the questions, hooray for you! You are well on your way to accepting yourself as you are. You probably have a great sex life and feel pretty darn good about yourself. Save your time—give this workbook to a friend.

"Yes" on four to eight:

If you answered yes on four to eight of the questions, you're on your way to loving the body you were born with. You probably feel confident about your body part of the time but very uneasy about it at others. Working through the exercises in this workbook will help you solidify your positive feelings about your body.

"Yes" on nine or more:

If your "yes" column is full of check marks, then this workbook is for you. It is the result of years of research and work with women of all shapes, sizes, and ages. In fact, during the years I've been counseling women, the recurrent themes are feelings of sadness, degradation, and hostility toward the body they were born with. So prevalent are these feelings that researchers now label negative body image as "normative discontent" in our culture. In other words, you are perfectly normal if you do not like your body.

Would you really be happy if you were thinner?

"If I were thin, I'd be totally happy!"

Have you ever said those words? Thought them? Believed them? I have heard them a thousand times, from women of all ages and sizes and backgrounds. If there were a university class called Happiness, I suspect millions of American women would expect the prerequisite for enrollment to read "*Must* be thin."

Throughout this book we are going to expend a lot of mental energy working on how to be happy, self-fulfilled women who love the bodies we were born with. Because the idea that thinness somehow equals happiness pervades our society, we must first dispose of that dangerous myth once and for all.

Where are our future leaders? In the bathroom, puking their guts out.

Nowhere is the evidence of this more compelling than on our university campuses, where we would expect to find the bright young women who will lead us into the future with their youthful energy and boundless enthusiasm. What do we find instead? Almost 20 percent of these women are starving themselves to death! Another 50 percent are vomiting their guts out in the university's bathrooms. Many of the "normal" ones are out running endless circles around the college track, trying to burn up the chicken bouillon they sipped for dinner.

During the ten years I spent counseling college students, I watched "erratic eating behaviors" mushroom into an epidemic so mind-boggling that the public health literature now calls it equivalent in seriousness to AIDS. I can vouch for the validity of that claim:

The pursuit of thinness is a deadly disease.

> *I have stared into the hollow eyes of a catatonic young woman who subsisted on half a bagel a day while practicing gymnastics for three hours every day.*
>
> *I have held the dried and withered hand of a twenty-one-year-old who ran ten miles a day on two bowls of Special K with skim milk.*
>
> *I have hugged the shaking bodies of young women who drove endlessly from one gas station to another in the middle of the night, buying candy bars, eating them in the car, and throwing them up at the next stop.*
>
> *I have been awakened in the middle of the night by young women terrified by the seizures of vomiting they brought on themselves by swallowing Ipecac syrup.*
>
> *I have spoken loudly to university administrators who could not understand why every year they had to put new plumbing in the women's bathrooms adjacent to the dining hall.*
>
> *I have watched beautiful, bright young women die.*

Hunger claims even our best and our brightest as its victims.

It is hard to comprehend this enormous loss of creative and intellectual energy, but its impact cannot be underestimated. These young women do not have the energy or ability to lead us into the next century, because they are hungry!

Hunger has enormous power. It is so basic that it overrides all other human needs. How can anyone who is in a state of starvation or semistarvation be happy? Women who starve themselves in an effort to be thin may indeed be thin, but *they are not happy.* They are far more likely to be depressed, hysterical, and prone to angry outbursts. They have noticeably less of all kinds of things: energy, interest in work and friends, enjoyment of all things sexual and sensual.

Some are so hungry that about the only things that set them apart from those starving to death in Third World countries are that they have nice clothes and, when they can't stand their hunger for one more second, they have the resources to go on an eating binge.

Some theorists speculate that all this is the result of dysfunctional families. Baloney! When 60 to 80 percent of college women can't eat normally, it is not because all of those families are dysfunctional. It is because those women have been conditioned to look for ugliness, fat, and slight imperfections in their bodies. They have been brainwashed into believing thinness is more important than intelligence or achievement or hard work. Our Declaration of Independence promised "life, liberty, and the pursuit of happiness." Too many women are making a Declaration of *De*pendence by letting their single-minded "pursuit of thinness" throw off their ambitions, derail their careers, and make them hungry.

The pursuit of thinness often takes precedence over everything else.

As women, we have made many gains over the years, including putting a higher value on ourselves. We have fought hard to increase the self-esteem and worth of all women, but now we are letting the quest for thinness erode those gains. As we achieve more control, education, and financial independence in the world, we are also feeling more hungry, out of control, foolish, and sexually insecure in our own bodies. If we can be made to hate our thighs, perhaps it's not too farfetched to conclude we can be made to hate all of ourselves that is feminine.

We must stop this obsessive pursuit of thinness and refuse to let it be our standard. It subverts our energies. It seriously impairs our ability to function at anywhere even close to our potential. It makes us complacent. We need our power and energy to make positive changes in our lives. To move forward, we must refuse to strive for a ridiculous cultural ideal that leads to intense misery while holding out the false promise of happiness.

One of the serious side effects of this negative thinking has been the inability of many women to enjoy and revel in the gifts of their own sexuality. Several years ago, I developed a workshop to address this issue: "Under the Sheets: Food, Body Image, and Women's Sexuality." Women from all walks of life responded from their hearts, using the workshop as an open forum to discuss, often for the first time, their deep-rooted concerns about food and sexuality. For some, the experience was a powerful tool for personal change as they began to see their lives in new and different ways. Others were so angered by the depiction of our culture's ideals of femininity that they decided to work for societal change.

This workbook evolved from those workshops. It is designed to teach you how to love the body you were born with so you can feel beautiful and sensual and self-fulfilled. It can help you redirect all of the energy you have spent beating yourself up over failed diets to building a meaningful, happy life. For too long, we have let advertisers and corporations dictate what we should look like. It is time to take back our bodies. It is time to focus our minds on our positive, creative energies. And it is time to see the future with hope, recognizing that we are worthy individuals, capable of loving whatever kind of body we were born with.

Learn to feel beautiful and sensual and self-fulfilled.

Take a Long, Forgiving Look

Love yourself first and everything else falls into line.
You really have to love yourself to get anything done in this world.

—LUCILLE BALL

Take my clothes OFF???

The first step in your journey is to assess where you are right now. For many of you, this will be the hardest step because, when you do the "Body Image Assessment" later in this chapter, you are going to have to take off your clothes and take a long look at your naked body. I know most of you haven't done this for ages, but you've got to trust me here. You *need* to make friends with your body. To do that, you've got to know where you're starting.

What about Mom and Grandma?

You've also got to keep in mind that your basic body was genetically determined. There is no way around that fact. Your mother, grandmothers, aunts, and great-grandmothers all carried the genetic bone structure you now own. And many women inherit their fathers' shapes—broad shoulders, thick neck, running-back knees, and all.

Because bone size cannot be changed—no matter how much you diet and exercise—fantasizing that you could look like a bone-thin model when you come from large-bone stock is an exercise in futility. You've got to assess—and accept—your genetic heritage and let go of impossible dreams if you are ever going to learn to love your body.

What you see in the mirror is only part of the picture.

As you prepare mentally for your actual assessment, I want to stress that what you see in the mirror will be only part of the picture. Your actual body image encompasses far more than the visual. It includes how you feel about your body. It includes how you carry yourself. And it includes all of the messages you have received about your particular body throughout your life.

To make things clearer, I've attached labels to the four components that make up your body image:

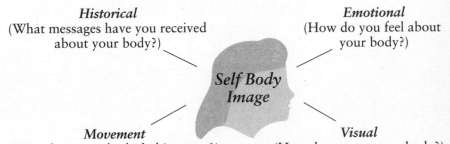

Historical
(What messages have you received about your body?)

Emotional
(How do you feel about your body?)

Self Body Image

Movement
(How does your body feel in space?)

Visual
(How do you see your body?)

Components of Body Image

The *visual* is the one you're used to—it's what reflects back at you when you stand in front of the mirror or catch yourself walking in front of a plate-glass store window.

The *emotional* part of body image covers your feelings about your body. Do you like some parts of your body—your hands, face, ankles, or hair? Do you feel a little critical about other parts—perhaps your breasts, knees, chin, or upper arms? Are you downright repulsed by other parts of your body—your thighs, abdomen, or pubic area, for example?

The *movement* aspect of body image is simply the way you carry yourself. Are you quick and light on your feet, or do you feel slow and cumbersome? Do you walk tall, or do you sort of slouch along? Do you sit up straight, or do you try to make yourself small?

The way to a man's heart is through his stomach . . .

The *historical* part of body image is the sum of all those messages you've been getting since you were born. Were you referred to as a chubby toddler? Did your brother laugh because you had freckles on your knees? Did the boys at the bus stop whistle when you walked by? Did your mother suggest you skip dessert and stress that no one would love you if you were fat? Did your grandmother tell you the way to a man's heart was through his stomach?

The sum of all these parts equals your body image. It begins with how you look, but spirals outward to take in how you think, move, act, carry yourself, and feel about yourself.

Ironically, men experience much less body dissatisfaction and distortion than women. We tend to overestimate our size. Studies conducted on normal-weight women with negative body images show exactly where to place the blame—on a society that places inordinate amounts of pressure on us to conform to a standard that totally ignores our individual biologies.

I hope that last remark filled you with outrage and courage, because it is now time to take a long look at your own body and figure out exactly where you stand in your own mind.

What do you see in the mirror?

Body Image Assessment (Part 1)

1. Take off your clothes (yes, all of them!). Turn up the lights and stand in front of a full-length mirror. As you look in the mirror, write down what you see:

Terrific parts: _____

Good parts: _____

Okay parts: _____

Bad parts: _____

Horrible parts: _____

continued

2. Now, while you are standing there, write down how you *feel* about what you are looking at. What kinds of thoughts do you have about your body? Instead of thinking in terms of good or bad, try to identify feelings like shame, pride, revulsion, happiness, sadness, sexiness, anxiety, disgust, detachment, and embarrassment.

_____

_____

_____

_____

Are you angry at your ancestors?

3. As you look at your naked body, try to picture your ancestors—your mother, her sisters, your grandmothers, and others. Try to identify which parts of your body are directly attributable to genetics:

_____

_____

_____

_____

You can now go ahead and get dressed. Find a quiet spot where you won't be disturbed and take Part II of the Body Image Assessment.

Body Image Assessment (Part II)

Are you a swan or an ostrich?

4. Picture yourself in an aerobics class or, if you've never been to one, dancing at a night club. (If you've never done either, you can imagine yourself walking down the supermarket aisle!) How

continued

does your body feel as it moves through space? Do you feel agile and in control, or do you feel clumsy and awkward? Does your body respond to what you tell it to do, or does it have a mind of its own? Is it graceful or clumsy, like an ostrich trying to fly? Try to describe in one or two sentences how your body feels when it's moving:

_____

_____

_____

_____

5. Now read the following section. Close your eyes, lean back your head, and take some deep, relaxing breaths.

What kind of little girl were you?

Picture yourself as a young girl, perhaps five or six. What kinds of messages do you remember hearing about your body?

- Were you praised for being a good eater or criticized for being a picky one?
- Were you taunted with "Fatty, fatty, two by four" or "Skinny, skinny, two by one"?
- Did anyone comment on your baby fat or beanpole legs?
- Were you praised for your ability to turn somersaults and hang by your knees or laughed at for bungling hopscotch?

Write down the most memorable messages from your childhood:

_____

_____

_____

continued

Were your teen years ghastly or great?

Now envision yourself as a young teen. You have just hit puberty. What kinds of messages, spoken or subtle, did other people give you about your body? What were your feelings about your body during this time when it was changing almost daily?

- Did you think you would die of embarrassment the first time (or every time!) you had to take a group shower in P.E. class?
- Were you excited or ashamed when you tried on your first bra?
- Did anyone comment on the size of your breasts or thighs or midriff?
- Did your brother tease you about the pimples on your back?

Write down the most memorable messages from your early teens:

_____

_____

_____

Did your best friend ever suggest Weight Watchers?

Now call to mind how you felt about your body when you were a young woman. What kind of feedback were your friends and family giving you?

- Did your best friend suggest you try Weight Watchers?
- Did your mate sabotage your diet efforts by bringing home your favorite pizza or dessert on the second day of your new diet?
- Did a sales clerk eye you disapprovingly, implying *her* clothes weren't for the likes of you?

continued

Write down the most memorable messages from these years:

_____

_____

_____

6. Read through all of the comments you made in this section. Try to summarize briefly how you feel about your body.

_____

_____

_____

Were you pretty hard on yourself, or did you find you were already starting to make friends with your body? Regardless of how you felt during this assessment, you need to keep the thoughts you had while you were doing it near the surface of your mind. They will be powerful tools in the quest to help you learn to see yourself in a more positive light.

What You Can Do Right Now

Get out old pictures of your ancestors and look at the genetic body makeup in your family. Think about all of the positive traits you received from your ancestors—your tenacity, your beautiful hair color, your ability to speak your mind. Before you move on to the next step, you need to *forgive your ancestors* and remind yourself that you were born with just this one body. Then promise yourself that you will work hard to learn how to love and nurture it.

Recognize How You've Been Duped

Let me listen to me and not to them.

—GERTRUDE STEIN

Representations of the "ideal" body keep changing.

Have you ever wandered through an art museum and thought how fat the women depicted in all those paintings and frescoes looked? "Rubenesque" we sometimes call them, after Flemish painter Peter Paul Rubens, whose idea of feminine beauty immortalized generous proportions. Some three hundred years later, Marilyn Monroe embodied perfection, yet by today's standards, even she looks a bit pudgy. It's not too hard to figure out why. When the "ideal" is the "waif" or the stick-figure model so popular on today's fashion runways and magazine covers, just about everyone else looks fat.

Even Marilyn Monroe!

No one likes to admit she's been duped, but think about it for a minute. Who decided that super-thin equaled beautiful? Did anyone ask for your vote? To say we've been sold a bill of goods is to put it mildly, with the emphasis on the word *sold*. Why else would we let the people who sell us things decide how we should look? Factor food and sex into the equation, and you can begin to see how we got stuck with an unattainable cultural ideal designed to keep us spending money and feeling dissatisfied for the rest of our lives.

Eat, eat, eat . . . but be slim, slim, slim!

Billboard-size cheeseburgers awaken our salivary glands and tempt us to eat even when we're not hungry. Full-color photos of calorie-laden desserts beckon from the magazine stand. Happy, healthy peo-

16

ple eat, eat, eat in television commercials, only to be replaced by slim, beautiful women encouraging us to alter our hair color, change our deodorant, or try a new toilet cleaner—implying we, too, can experience a higher level of being if we are thin and follow their advice. Want to look sexy? Just buy a particular brand of jeans, liquor, cigarettes, or cereal.

Obvious, slick ploys—yet we fall for them. Why? Because we are vulnerable. Images of food, beauty, and sex permeate every niche of our lives. For as long as most of us can remember, we've been bombarded with messages about what our bodies should look like, what we should eat, and how we should feel. Is it any wonder we got suckered?

To love the body you were born with, you have to get beyond the often contradictory media messages that have been dogging you all your life. Begin with a detached look at some of the most insidious ways others are masterminding how you feel about yourself.

Eating Behavior and Body Image Messages Targeted at Children

Our children are innocent prey as well.

Most preschoolers don't know the difference between a nickel and a quarter, much less a one-dollar bill and a twenty. Unfortunately, that doesn't keep them from being the targets of multimillion-dollar advertising campaigns paid for by the food and toy industries.

The stakes are huge. If a kid can talk, she can put pressure on Mom or Dad to spend money. Number crunchers estimate that a walloping 40 percent of a typical family's food dollars are influenced by children, both through requests at the grocery store and preferences for certain fast-food restaurants. If you have children, you know firsthand how powerful the "kiddie" commercials can be when it comes to food choices.

This was drummed into me when I took my four-year-old son grocery shopping and he started begging me to buy a certain type of fruit snack.

"Why?" I asked him. I hadn't bought it before and was pretty sure he'd never even tasted it. He told me in all seriousness that this particular fruit snack could make him fly—he had seen it on television!

If kids believe certain foods can make them fly, imagine how gullible they are when it comes to the real message: certain foods will make them *happy*. Is it any wonder childhood obesity is now a major medical problem?

But influencing eating behavior is only half of the picture. Advertisements aimed at children also strongly tout toys. If you question for even one second the power these commercials wield, I have a story for you. Every Christmas, my friend with four school-age kids would ask her children to make a wish list. Each list always included several toys. The father of this family was in the army, and eventually they all ended up overseas, where American television was limited to the Armed Forces Network—which airs no commercials. When Christmas rolled around, none of the children had the slightest idea what toys to request!

The impact of such powerful mind manipulation on body image cannot be overstressed, since the top-selling toys on the market today represent thoroughly fictitious images of what adult men and women look like.

Does your daughter look like Barbie? Did you?

More than 90 percent of girls three to eleven years old own at least one Barbie doll. When Barbie's proportions are translated into "real-life" numbers, her measurements are 38–21–36. How many women do you know with such a figure? Probably none! Those particular dimensions are virtually unattainable in adulthood.

Keep in mind that Barbie comes with hordes of high-fashion clothes and accessories. She also has Ken. The inevitable result is that young girls start believing the ultimate figure and the latest fashions will ensure their popularity, especially with the opposite sex.

The message sent to boys is not much nicer. G.I. Joe, the top-selling boys' toy for the last twenty years, is just as surreal as Barbie. With his bulky biceps, thin waist, and rippled abdomen, he is portrayed as the "All-American" hero. The equipment G.I. Joe carries on his back would actually weigh 200–250 pounds!

Commercials for these two toys and countless others give our children very clear mental pictures of how a "real man" and an "ideal woman" should look in our culture. The fact that they cannot possibly measure up later in life simply does not matter.

The Teen Years: You Are What You Look

Being thin is in.

Did you ever wonder what the key to being part of your high school's "in" group was? Probably not, because the answer is fairly obvious: you have to look the part. Body, clothes, hair—they're all components of the all-important image that determine "in" and "out." For teenagers trying to figure out who they are in an already confusing world, one media message comes through loud and clear: in your peers' eyes—the only ones that really matter here—you are what you look.

Total emaciation . . . the ultimate in thin.

About the worst thing a girl can be in junior high or high school is overweight—by her peers' standards. The glamorization of thinness, though, has passed all reasonable bounds. Otherwise healthy kids, who may even still be growing, go on starvation diets. Anorexia nervosa has reached epidemic proportions as more and more teens strive for the ultimate in thin: total emaciation. Even teens who look and seem perfectly normal believe they are not thin enough, and the seeds of "normative discontent" with their bodies start growing faster than Jack's bean stalk.

In order to understand the severity of this pressure, pay a visit to your local high school at lunch time. Stand by and watch what teenage girls call "lunch" today. It is not "cool" to be seen eating in public anymore, especially at school. Competition reigns to be the one to eat the smallest amount of food, if any. I have watched three girls share one candy bar, each taking tiny nibbles to ensure they do not appear too hungry. Virtuous stories are whispered of unending days without food or meals, always to be outdone by another who has survived longer with less.

When researchers asked teenage girls to describe their "ideal" body, the overwhelming favorite looked like this:

Guess who this description fits?

Height: 5'7"
Size: 5
Weight: 110 pounds
Big blue eyes
Long blonde hair

All that advertising aimed at children finally paid off. As teens, most girls still want to look just like Barbie.

Standing in stark contrast to the glamorization of thinness are all those messages that equate food with fun. Pizza parties, burger hangouts, mall meals: food is a huge part of a teenager's social life. For every media message equating beauty with thinness, there's another commercial designed to convince teens that food will make them happy.

When I was teaching nutrition at a university and regularly counseling older teens, I heard countless stories of "binge parties" involving whole groups who would gather in one girl's dorm room, order pizzas and cart in huge supplies of junk food, then eat the night away. When the food was gone, they would secretly steal away to the communal toilets and stick fingers down their throats, purging the "bad" food that had made them happy for a few moments.

More dual messages.

So extraordinary were the pressures resulting from the dual messages of eating for happiness and staying slim for happiness that most of these girls considered vomiting "okay" behavior. Many of them actually felt rather virtuous because they engaged in such behavior only occasionally, not every day or several times a day like the "real" bulimics they knew.

These girls repeatedly cycle through denying food and then bingeing large amounts to rid themselves of anxiety and depression, to express powerlessness, and to restore a sense of control in their lives. As girls in our society, they are not allowed the luxury of turning their anger outward, and so the only outlet for their rage is their own body. The relief is merely temporary, and the circumstances that prompted the behavior remain unchanged.

The often destructive relationship between food and appearance is clear, but the whole question of sexuality belongs in the picture, too. Teenage pregnancy rates are soaring, and the message still coming across is "everyone" is doing "it." In the movies and on television, as well as in ads, the implied message is that the attractive, slim female gets the man. The mystique surrounding sex at this age is only compounded by the secrecy and covert attitudes most adults have about communicating openly with teens on sexual issues.

Young Adults: Genetic Freaks Embody the "Ideal"

Only 2 percent of women can ever attain a model-thin body.

As a member of the scientific community, I have always found it ironic that most biological scientists consider the young-adult women portrayed as "ideal" by the media to actually be "genetic freaks." In many instances these super-thin models are unable to propagate the human race because of infertility and lack of regular menstrual cycles brought on by their extremely low body-fat percentage. Yet somehow the 2 percent of the population born with thin, bony bodies are held up to the other 98 percent of us as the American ideal.

Advertisements targeting young adults almost always feature these very thin young women with perfect makeup, perfect hair, perfect nails, perfect clothes or very few clothes or even no clothes—ad nauseam. The message is that the young woman who has all these things gets the man. I guess it never occurred to those ad-executive types that snagging a mate might *not* be the primary goal for some of us!

Unfortunately, slimness is also equated with professional success. If you don't have the self-discipline to keep yourself trim, how could you possibly exhibit self-discipline in the workplace? This double whammy makes young women very vulnerable to peer-group standards, often leading to negative consequences in their personal as well as their professional lives.

How many can diet their way to perfection?

This is especially true for young women who began dieting as teenagers and still have negative thoughts about their bodies. No matter how much they achieve or how hard they work, they come up short in their own minds. As a result, they expend their energy pleasing others. They know from countless failed efforts at trying to diet their way to perfection that they are doomed to failure. Often, they try to compensate by looking for perfection in a mate.

Since none of us is perfect, this search, too, is probably doomed. A common reaction, especially if the man is the one terminating the relationship: "I wasn't thin enough." Even if the "dumping" was due in large part to the woman's preoccupation with dieting and thinness, she is still likely to blame her size. It never occurs to her that the man of her dreams may be looking for someone who loves the body she was born with and has a confident, positive world view.

Research has provided us with some interesting insights into this phenomenon. Although women repeatedly overestimate their own body size, they also *underestimate* the size they feel is attractive to men. Male college students have been found to rate the body size of their ideal woman as significantly larger than what women assume men desire. These men did not prefer the emaciated, bone-thin women but images of women that were well proportioned and well rounded.

Finding their own identity and unique place in the world are the most important developmental goals for young adults. Self-respect is an essential part of the process. We all need to believe in our right to be happy. We need to believe we deserve success, friendship, and love. Focusing on media messages gives us an external, inaccurate, inadequate view of who we should really be. It is almost impossible to establish healthy, positive relationships until we first respect ourselves.

Have you been Scotch-taped lately?

Another problem with media messages targeted at young adults is that they underline the mind-body split. Most ads depict a perfect set of thighs, a hand full of long, pretty nails, or a perfect, blemish-free face. We assume the model is a wholly beautiful person judging only from the small part we see. When women are photographed in their entirety, they are often taped (yes, Scotch-taped!) together so their breasts and fannies are uplifted. Models routinely report how their bodies, the lights, the wind, and the cameras are all manipulated to make them look ideal. And after all that, the photographs are almost always retouched.

Now imagine living on eight ounces of yogurt a day or spending five hours a day at the gym, as some of these models do. Why is it so difficult to believe we can *never* look like these women?

Where did they hide all the size 12s?

Yet many of my young-adult clients over the years *still* think they should be able to look like the models. They cite proof of their inadequacy as the fact that stores are always full of size 4 and size 6 clothing, which they, of course, can no longer wear. I personally think this is the one area where we get our revenge—all of the good stuff that fits normal women sells out quickly, and the big boys have to take a loss on the stuff meant for those "ideal" bodies!

Happily Married? Prepare for Perfection Pressure!

Once a woman "finds her man" and settles into some type of permanent relationship, she immediately faces an entirely new onslaught of problems and concerns dreamed up by a media more eager than ever to share her dollars.

Here is the societal standard she is expected to live up to:

Guide to the perfect woman.

1. Birth children while maintaining a svelte body.
2. Prepare family feasts while staying thin.
3. Reward herself with sweets and other food treats without gaining weight.
4. Exercise often and keep the old sex life hopping without succumbing to fatigue.

What is the implied penalty for failing to live up to these confusing, contradictory standards? Losing the man, of course. If you believe the media messages, there are hordes of young, slim women waiting in the wings for your husband. "Don't hate me because I'm beautiful" is one of the more obvious, obnoxious commercials along this line.

Hormones play a part, too.

Now consider the facts. Estrogen and progesterone, the hormones required to conceive and bear children, are both fat producing and fat hoarding. Pregnancy itself is fattening, producing metabolic changes that make gaining weight almost inevitable. Raising kids takes a lot of time and even more energy. How can we find the time for regular exercise? Who has time to act, much less feel, sexy? In many marriages, the combination of hormone imbalances, fatigue, and childbirth can just about kill a couple's sex life!

Feed your family, but don't you dare eat!

A central task in nurturing a family includes feeding them. In generations past, feeding the family was a primary source of internal pride for women. Today it is a primary source of guilt. How do you prepare healthy, well-balanced meals after putting in ten hours at the office? In addition to ads telling us how we should look and feel, we've also got to deal with those telling us what "good" mothers feed their families. Check out the current covers of women's magazines and the dilemma becomes even clearer: pictured on the front are gooey, fatty desserts "your family will love" juxtaposed with a couple of lines touting the latest fad diet designed to help you lose ten inches or ten pounds in ten days.

Perhaps the most offensive messages are those that mock our limited time, privacy, and energy stores. I personally detest those ads that picture a woman alone with her ice cream or other tantalizing dessert. The message is always "I deserve this during *my* time." That is about as explicit as you can get without coming right out and saying sweets can replace sex.

It also implies that while women are allowed to prepare the food, they dare not eat openly. Next time you are out for lunch; check out the other women: how many actually watch the dessert tray being presented, and how many simply watch what the others will order instead?

Save Your Gold for Those Happy, Golden Years

Grandma's not safe anymore, either. She's supposed to look like Cher.

Once upon a time, postmenopausal women could be content with their changing bodies. The "grandmotherly" look was a beloved one. Today, the pressure to be thin does not necessarily ease with the passing of the years. The advertising industry and the media have women like Cher, Jane Fonda, and Linda Evans to present pictures of how "older" women should look. Reference is seldom made to the number of plastic surgeries and tremendous expense required to maintain this lithe look!

On the bright side, many mature women are finally abandoning the struggle for an impossible-to-achieve body. Through a growing awareness of themselves and a lifetime of experiences to back them up, they are finally able to see ludicrous media messages for what they are.

The New Advertising: Muscling in on Your Dollars

Extreme fitness, extreme thinness—poor measures of a woman's worth!

One of the newer trends in advertising is to feature strong, determined, highly fit women who are "just doing it." I have heard many comments about the focus being shifted from super-thin models to more athletic ones, at least in athletic-shoe commercials. As a more muscular and healthy ideal competes with the super-thin one, we can expect both a positive and a negative impact. On the plus side, we can all benefit physically and psychologically from regular exercise. On the down side, extreme fitness is not much different from extreme thinness as a measure of a woman's beauty and worth. It is merely a slightly different way of applying pressure on women to control and master their bodies. To complete this new picture of goodness and beauty, you must add compulsive exercising to the already established virtues of self-discipline and continuous dieting.

What You Can Do Right Now

Admit that you've been duped, and vow you won't fall for the same old media trap again. When you see ludicrous commercials or advertisements that portray totally unrealistic pictures of women's bodies and lives, *cast your vote* by boycotting those products. Never buy anything that glamorizes or encourages anorexia and bulimia by featuring emaciated models. If we all wrote letters to the presidents of these companies, our voices would gather strength. We *can* make a difference if we all act together!

Kick the Diet Habit

Never eat more than you can lift.

—MISS PIGGY

The first problem for all of us, men and women, is not to learn, but to unlearn.

—GLORIA STEINEM

Does it sometimes feel as if you've spent your entire adult life either on a diet or a binge? Over the years, I've counseled hundreds of women who had easily lost over a thousand pounds each. Unfortunately, they kept losing the same ten or twenty or even fifty pounds over and over and over.

Up and down the scales, like a worn-out piano.

One of my favorite clients referred to herself as a worn-out piano because of the many trips she'd made up and down the scale. She weighed herself every single morning and measured her worth by the feedback the scale gave her. Over the years, she had tried every diet she could find: the grapefruit diet, the Scarsdale diet, the only-fruit-in-the-morning diet, the all-meat diet, an 800-calorie-a-day diet, a 1,500-calorie-a-day diet, and countless others.

She was a veteran of Weight Watchers and Overeaters Anonymous and several diet centers that left both her pocketbook and her body substantially lighter. She succeeded at everything, for a while. But as soon as she reached her goal and went off whatever diet she'd been on, the result was always the same: she started gaining weight again. Many times she ended up heavier than she'd been when she started.

The cave woman's famine is the modern woman's diet.

To understand why this kind of chronic dieting doesn't work, take a look at one of our cave-dwelling ancestors. Although this cave woman certainly didn't choose to diet, she was forced to endure the equivalent during the long winters she spent holed up in a cave with her children, trying to survive on berries, nuts, leaves, and whatever else she had managed to accumulate during the summer and fall. She also "dieted" during what were sometimes very long periods of drought and famine.

When food was scarce, two important things happened in this woman's body that helped ensure the survival of our species. First, her metabolic rate slowed down, helping her body conserve fat for later use. Second, her anxiety level rose in direct proportion to her need for food. Even in the dead of winter, this "hypothalamus response" could motivate her to get out of her warm cave and go hunt for food.

Our bodies are still back in the cave.

Women whose bodies were not so efficient at storing fat and women without a strong hypothalamus urging them to eat *died*. As women, we all descended from the efficient fat storers with the strong "hypo-thalamus response." In fact, our bodies still function much as they did back in the cave. Whenever we withhold food, they start hoarding energy. When we've been hungry long enough, they tell us to get out there and hunt. The fact that our hunting grounds are our own refrigerators and the aisles of the local supermarket has yet to make its marks on our evolutionary development.

As our cave woman ancestor illustrates, the diet game is a very hard one to play because the deck was stacked against us a few millennia ago. She knew all along that the stakes were life and death, but we've only recently realized that those who play the diet game are playing with the same high stakes. The "winners" may be thin for a while, but the losers sometimes die.

Why are we creating famines?

If we are going to love the bodies we were born with, we must stop putting them through artificially created famines. We must feed them plenty of healthy, nutritious food so they can function at their peak all year round. To do this, we must change our attitudes about dieting and weight on both the individual and societal levels. The best starting place to effect such change is with an examination of our own atti-tudes toward dieting and weight loss.

Dieting and Weight Loss: An Attitude Checklist

1. I've wanted to lose weight since my

___ Childhood   ___ Adolescence   ___ Late teens

___ Young adulthood   ___ Motherhood   ___ Mature years

___ Other_____

Pick your prehistoric season.

2. My current attitude about my weight compares best to

___ Winter ("Stick me in the cave and starve me!")

___ Spring ("Let me out of the cave. I'm hungry!")

___ Summer ("I'm doing fine—getting lots of food and exercise.")

___ Fall ("I've stored enough fat to see me through the winter.")

3. I have put my body through_____periods of self-induced famine.   (# of diets you've been on)

Who wants you to be thin?

4. The reason I keep going on diets and trying to lose weight is that I feel pressure (spoken or unspoken) to be thin (or at least less fat) from (check all that apply)

___ Other women in my age group

___ My spouse or partner (past or present)

___ My desire to attract friends, dates, or a future partner

___ My children

___ My parent(s)

___ My siblings or other family members

___ My job or career

___ Myself

___ Other_____

Has dieting made you happy?

Take a close look at your answers to those four questions. Have your dieting efforts made your life any happier? Have they made anyone else in your life any happier? If you are like most of us, they have led to a lot of misery for a lot of years! In addition to a whole host of medical problems associated with yo-yo weight gains and losses, constant dieting produces frustration, a sense of failure, poor self-esteem, an empty wallet, and negative self-views.

To love the body you were born with, you need to completely and dramatically change your attitudes and fundamental beliefs about your weight. For starters, you must *stop* abusing your body. And that is just what dieting is: abuse!

Remember to hunt for buffalo.

Now, before you toss this workbook in the garbage because you'd been secretly hoping it held the key to your next dieting success, I want to tell you the odds are good you will lose weight and keep it off forever once you start loving your body—*if you need to lose weight.* When you love your body, you are motivated to take good care of it. That includes feeding it often, throughout the day and not letting it think for one minute that it is about to face another famine. That also means coming out of your cave and doing some daily hunting—the kind where you walk, run, climb, push, pull, swim, and *move,* not the kind where you open the kitchen cupboard!

What were all those years of deprivation for, anyway?

Still, if dieting has been a big part of your life, it may be hard to let it go. What were all those years of deprivation for, anyway? What were all those diet books and guides and calorie/gram counters for? If you are like most chronic dieters, you have amassed a whole storehouse of diet-related information, so let's just take a minute here to test your "Diet I.Q."

Fact or Myth? The Diet I.Q. Quick Quiz

1. All calories are created equal.
2. Cutting calories will result in weight loss.
3. When it comes to risk factors for fat-related diseases, the location of fat on the body is more important than how much fat there is.

4. Regular exercise doesn't account for much weight loss compared to dieting.
5. Skipping meals will help reduce weight quickly.
6. Weighing yourself every day will help you control your weight.

#1. ALL CALORIES ARE CREATED EQUAL.

True, but . . . a calorie is a calorie is a calorie. It is a unit of heat energy regardless of the food source. Three hundred calories of watermelon is the same as three hundred calories of chocolate ice cream. But . . . fat contains more than twice the number of calories per gram that proteins and carbohydrates do. In addition, it takes about *eight* times as many calories to digest and convert complex carbohydrates such as fruit, vegetables, grains, and rice into body fat as it does to digest and convert dietary fat into body fat. This is the main reason low-fat eating is much more successful than low-calorie eating. Your body can use and burn lots more calories when they come from fruits, vegetables, grains, and legumes.

For example, if you eat a potato, your body will burn a fair amount of the potato calories just in the digestion process alone. The remaining potato calories will "hang out" in your system for a while waiting for you to use them. But if you pile butter or sour cream on that potato, the fat will digest and become body fat with little effort—very few of the calories in fats get burned in the digestion process.

#2. CUTTING CALORIES WILL RESULT IN WEIGHT LOSS.

True, you may lose weight, but it probably won't be much fat.

This basic premise underlies most of the diets we embark on. Unfortunately, it is far from the true picture. There are numerous reasons for this.

Many researchers believe that our bodies have natural "set points" or plateaus that help in maintaining our body weight at a certain level. Once we drop below this body weight, our survival mechanisms kick into high gear in order to prevent the loss of additional weight. Some of these mechanisms include the strong hypothalamic response we saw in the cave woman earlier, sending her out in search of food. The body also tends to slow down physical output, partly because of the decrease in calories available and partly because of built-in hormonal mechanisms.

Consider the example of a woman who decides to start a weight loss diet with a 1,000-calorie-a-day deficit. In seven days, she would reduce her total calorie consumption by 7,000 calories. During the first week she would have lost carbohydrate stores, which the body likes to give up first, along with some fat and a considerable amount of water stores. Assuming she maintained this level, she *should* continue to lose one pound every three and a half days. But this operates under the assumption that the body's calorie needs will continue to match her current output. What happens when she becomes lethargic through the absence of so many calories?

Another important fact is that the calorie cost of her physical activities continues to decrease as she loses body mass. It takes more calories to move a 200-pound woman walking down the street than a 150-pound woman. Her calorie needs will drop accordingly.

These biological responses to dieting account in part for the fact that while she may have lost three or four pounds during the first week of her diet, she loses almost nothing on the exact same diet a few weeks later. In our culture, we tend to accuse the dieter of cheating when this happens or, if we are the dieter, we blame the diet and switch to a new one. Since there are so many diets floating around, this is not a problem!

This also assumes that she will persevere with this drastically reduced calorie intake in spite of social engagements, her gnawing stomach, and increased fatigue until her desired body size is achieved. Rarely does this happen.

Eventually, the urge to eat wins out and her weight is regained. If she is not exercising during this regain period, she regains fat and not the higher calorie burner that muscle is. The next time she attempts to restrict caloric intake without exercise, she starts with a higher percent of body fat and a lower amount of muscle, making the weight loss that much more difficult.

Many women have come to my office over the years, swearing that they are subsisting on minimal amounts of food and calories. They look aghast when I tell them I believe them! Others have assumed that these people have been in their closets stuffing down food, but instead their bodies have played cruel tricks on them. Endless weight reduction diets over the years without regular exercise programs have resulted in efficient bodies that are trained to store all the available calories they are given. A high body fat percentage with a low muscle mass has added to the problem. Because body fat requires fewer calories for maintenance compared to muscle tissue, they require only a minimal amount of calories to maintain their weight.

Another fact useful in dispelling this myth concerns the loss of body fat. Many people assume that if they lose weight, they lose body fat. Sad news, but our bodies don't work that way. Weight reduction in an adult occurs by a decrease in the *size* of the fat cell, not the *number* of cells. In other words, they can shrink but they don't disappear! Consider them lying in wait for your next urge for that chocolate ice cream. This is a pessimistic outlook for the obese person who hopes to stay permanently reduced, and explains in part why so few people are successful in long-term weight loss. It is also one of the biggest arguments for the need to engage in regular exercise. Exercise helps balance your appetite controls, and additional muscle mass helps burn the chocolate ice cream calories.

The positive side of this dilemma is the need for prevention of obesity in our children. Children who grow into adulthood without these excess fat cells typically have an easier time keeping weight off in adulthood than do children who are obese. Healthy eating and exercise behaviors begun in childhood can prevent a lifetime struggle against these stubborn fat cells.

#3. WHEN IT COMES TO RISK FACTORS FOR FAT-RELATED DISEASES, THE LOCATION OF FAT ON THE BODY IS MORE IMPORTANT THAN HOW MUCH FAT THERE ACTUALLY IS.

The fact that huge numbers of Americans are overweight is an increasing concern to the medical community. Because some types of obesity do present health risks for some individuals, we have accepted as fact that any type of excess weight is automatically bad for everyone. In many cases, however, this is simply not true, especially for women.

The female, estrogen-based fat pattern—that "pear" shape so many of us hate—is associated with fewer health risks. As many of us know firsthand, the greatest proportion of fat in this body type is stored in the hips and thighs. The good news is that fat concentrated in those two spots is not related to as high a level of disease risk as the male pattern of obesity. The bad news is that fat cells in the hips and thighs store fat easily and give it up begrudgingly, except during breast-feeding. Also, this estrogen protection is lost after menopause, when women's risks become equal to men's.

Male-pattern obesity—the "apple" shape—is associated with substantially higher risks for many medical problems: cardiovascular disease, hypertension, diabetes, and cancer are some of the more researched conditions. The apple shape implies health risks at even modest levels of obesity for both men *and* women carrying the majority of their excess fat above their waist.

Humans carry two types of fat on their bodies: essential fat and storage fat. Essential fat is stored in the marrow of the bones as well as in the heart, lungs, liver, spleen, and other organs. This fat is required for normal body functioning and helps support these organs within the body. Gender-specific fat, or the fat *essential* to female functions, is located in the breasts and pelvis. This fat helps maintain normal female hormonal functions such as menstruation and also provides the calories to support childbirth and breast-feeding. Women have three times the essential fat of males to ensure our species continues.

Sadly, this is the fat that so many of my clients over the years have found disgusting. They eye their curvaceous female body in the mirror with sadness and anger, falsely thinking that they can change this biological fact of life. Washboard abdomens are nearly impossible for most women. The few who can achieve this look spend four to five hours a day in the gym and live on nearly fat-free diets for weeks prior to their competitions.

Have you ever stopped to think how much *room* it takes just to store our uterus, fallopian tubes, and cervix? The next time you get disgusted with your inability to have a perfectly flat stomach, think about how much space this female "equipment" requires in our abdomens. This doesn't mean that women shouldn't do abdominal exercises; strong abdominals provide support to the entire body, especially the lower back. But be realistic in your expectations of what you find successful!

Storage fat is another matter. This fat is stored as "adipose" tissue and is available for energy use should we ever need it. (The problem for many Americans is that we rarely get the chance to dip into *this* savings account!) The body hoards these stores and gives them up only with a fight, such as during prolonged exercise or long-term fasting.

There is no denying the fact that excess body fat increases the risk of disease for some people with some types of bodies. It is important to determine what type of fat you have and where you have it. An easy way for you to determine this yourself is to do a simple test called the "Waist-to-Hip Ratio."

1. Measure your waist with a tape measure at your navel while standing relaxed, being sure not to "suck it in."
2. Measure around your hips, over your buttocks where you are the widest.
3. Divide your waist measure by your hip measure.

If the number you come up with is greater than .80, you are probably an "apple" and at greater risk of obesity-related diseases. Males who exceed .95 for this ratio are also at higher risk. If your waist-to-hip ratio is less than .80, you are probably a "pear" and may have lower risk of diseases related to excess body fat.

#4. REGULAR EXERCISE DOESN'T ACCOUNT FOR MUCH WEIGHT LOSS COMPARED TO DIETING.

For years I have watched women repeatedly rob their bodies of essential nutrients and energy under the guise of dieting and weight loss. These same women, living on grapefruit and cottage cheese, will avoid regular exercise at all costs. They drive around the grocery store parking lot for fifteen minutes looking for a parking space to avoid a 500-yard walk to the front door!

Dieting without a regular exercise program promises only short-term results, rarely resulting in maintenance of weight loss longer than six months. Of 29 million serious dieters in the United States in 1991, 20.6 million were female. For these women, 630 million pounds were lost and 489 million pounds regained. Researchers estimate that up to 98 percent of dieters gain back the weight they have lost within three years. The sad part of this story is that a majority of those dieters regain their original weight, *plus* an additional 20 percent! Not good odds, considering the effort, energy, and turmoil dieting causes in most people's lives. We all know women who have gone to their neighborhood dieting center and shed incredible amounts of weight before our eyes, only to be seen a year later heavier than when they started.

These women have still not learned the remarkable secrets of exercise. Their bodies are operating under that cave woman's survival system, reducing weight during the famine periods and storing up quickly when the harvest season is upon them.

Consider what happens when daily calorie intake exceeds what a woman is burning. This could result from eating just one extra banana every day. Over a year's time, this would amount to an excess of 36,500 calories. This would result in almost a five-pound weight gain in one year. On the other hand, if she eliminated one tablespoon of butter or margarine and walked one mile every day, she would lose approximately 21 pounds in the same year!

This would occur partly because of the high concentration of calories found in fat foods and in part because of her increased energy output. Exercise is believed to raise the "set point" discussed earlier, conserving and even increasing lean body mass. It raises your resting metabolism and helps enzymes that aid in fat breakdown in your tissues.

Regular exercise also helps women psychologically to feel better about themselves and their bodies. It gives us a sense of power and control over our body, helping to connect with both our inner spiritual senses and our outer world as well. Ask women who exercise regularly why they continue, and most often you will hear answers of this type.

One of the most important steps in learning to love the body you were born with is to begin using it: *move it!* Some people exercise vehemently, others on occasion, and still others never quite find the time.

In order to assess how you feel about exercise, take some time to think through and answer the following questions:

1. I exercise when . . .

_____

_____

_____

_____

2. I don't exercise when . . .

_____

_____

_____

_____

3. Exercise makes me feel:

___tired	___enthusiastic	___fat
___energetic	___old	___thin
___sore (muscles)	___in control	___powerful
___strong	___desirable	___disgusted
___other: _____		

4. The last time I exercised was_____.

5. I would exercise more, but . . .
   (List below all the reasons you don't exercise more than you do)

   a. _____

   b. _____

   c. _____

   d. _____

   e. _____

   f. _____

6. What activities do you *enjoy* doing? Think back to when you were a child. Were there activities during your childhood or teen years that really excited you? These may be the ones to begin your list with. Add to it those things that you have always wanted to try but haven't had the time to learn.

a. _____

b. _____

c. _____

d. _____

e. _____

The people I have seen over the years who begin an exercise program and stay with it through time are usually those who have a combination of different activities they enjoy. This keeps them from falling into a rut and getting bored with the same routine. It also helps their muscles adapt to different types of activities and results in more balanced training of their body.

Exercise has been a fundamental factor throughout my entire life. If I am traveling to do workshops or take a vacation, I always bring along a swim suit and a pair of walking shoes. This allows me to swim in the pool or, if one is unavailable, to walk the hallways of the hotel. Because my husband is often out of the country with the military for months at a time, I have had to learn to be creative in fitting full-time work, care of the children, and exercise into my life.

When I was pregnant with my sons, I stopped going to my high-impact aerobics classes and joined a Jazzercise group in my area that promised a less-jarring workout for my body. The sight of me in red and white striped leotards, nine months pregnant, struck panic and fear into my class partners! When my boys were in their early years I threw them into a backpack and hit the roads to walk. As they got older, I put them both in a bike trailer and pulled them with me on my errands. Now that they are older, I go for "bike walks" with them, where they bike along with me as I strut to keep pace with them. We often go to the pool and horseplay, or I swim laps while they are practicing their swimming lessons. Not only has exercise given me the energy to keep up with their active days, but it has also taught them that exercise and activity are an essential part of a healthy lifestyle. I strongly believe that anyone can exercise if she uses her creative energies to find a way to fit it into her life.

The most common excuse I have heard over the years for not exercising is simply not having the time. As you get into the next chapters we will begin to take a look at where your time goes and to what purposes. For now, suffice it to say that you don't have time *not* to exercise. Any exercise physiologist will tell you that regular exercise not only adds days to your life but life to your days. Regular activity results in having increased time in your day for the other goals and activities you want to pursue. The exchange of fresh oxygen in your cells revitalizes your body and adds energy to your every move. People who exercise regularly require less sleep, and therefore can add extra productive hours to their day. Not only will you not have to suffer those "after dinner blahs" when you are unable to lift yourself off the couch, but you will find yourself waking up in the morning less tired after less sleep.

For every fifteen minutes of exercise you do a day, you can estimate an additional hour of extra energy. This means that if you were to walk one-half hour every day, you would gain back the half hour you spent exercising *plus* an additional hour and a half of more productive time to do other things you enjoy.

Regular exercise is by far the surest way to tone your muscles, increase your muscle mass and calorie burning rate, and begin to get in touch with the body you were born with. It's not how hard you push or how sweaty you get that matters. Just push yourself up from the chair and out the door and do whatever activity it is you love. If you move and enjoy it, you will look and feel better than ever, and you won't miss the old dieting life one bit.

#5. SKIPPING MEALS WILL HELP REDUCE WEIGHT QUICKLY.

Unfortunately for many Americans, skipping meals is a sign of bravado and willpower. It is considered almost heroic to pass up breakfast and lunch under the guise of control. "I don't do breakfast" and "I can't take anything but coffee until noon" are commonly heard in our daily conversations. For some of you, this is because you like to begin each new day on a diet, trying to make up for eating too much the night before.

Our bodies have powerful mechanisms that kick in when they feel they have been underfed, encouraging us to eat more. If you skip breakfast and lunch often, you already know how this works. You begin snacking in the late afternoon and continue eating everything in sight through dinner and straight through to bed. The "fast" of the morning leads to a "binge" in the evening. It is the body's way of saying, "Okay, you jerk. You expected me to put out all day for you while you were busy, but now it is time to pay the piper!" The same principle applies when you go several days without eating much—as soon as you start to eat, your body signals you to keep eating to make up for the fast.

I challenge you to try something new. Feed your body the food it needs when it needs it. Eat some breakfast. If you are like the 80 percent of my clients who abhor the idea of breakfast, you may find something very interesting just as they do when they begin eating it—they are no longer as hungry in the evening. If the idea of food before noon makes your stomach curdle, you are seeing one more symptom of how disconnected your mind and body have become. Our bodies were not meant to go 15 hours or more without food; therefore the term "breakfast," meaning to break the fast.

Start with something small, such as a container of yogurt or a piece of fruit, within an hour or two of when you get up. Two hours or so later, add some graham crackers or a bowl of cereal. Eat a hearty lunch of soup and salad or sandwich and fruit. Try this for one week. Initially, you may feel ill at the thought of eating this early. But a strange thing happens to your body after the end of the first week or so. You will notice that you begin to feel hungry in the morning, yet quite satisfied at dinner time with a much smaller amount of food. Not only will this give your body the energy it needs for your output during the day, but you will also feel more energetic later into the evening because you are not filling yourself with lots of calories close to bedtime.

Eating small frequent meals of complex carbohydrates through-out the day is the answer. Your body becomes accustomed to being regularly fed and doesn't need to hoard the calories you would eat at one meal a day. Your energy level stays higher throughout the day when you need it, and your appetite and weight will begin to normalize.

#6. Weighing yourself every day will help you control your weight.

If you have been using your scale as an indicator of whether or not your dieting efforts are successful, now is the time to heave it into the garbage can. The scale is a worthless measure of weight fluctuations and can seriously damage your resolve to love the body you were born with.

1. If you are exercising regularly, you will lose fat mass and gain muscle mass, which weighs more. Therefore, the scale will not indicate your success. You *want* to lose fat and gain muscle, as muscle requires more calories than fat just to exist every second of every day. Remember, fat is a "metabolic parasite" and hangs on for the ride, requiring minimal calories to maintain itself.

Think about this! When is the last time someone walked up to you and said, "Oh, Jane, you look so great! You must be down to 125 pounds now!"? No way! No one but ourselves and maybe our Higher Power know those numbers staring back at us from the scale. Instead, people make comments such as, "Oh, Jane, you look so great! You are really getting in shape!" Why not use *that* as your goal instead of playing the numbers game?

2. Weight fluctuates daily, depending on what you've had to eat and drink, how much you've exercised, and what point you're at in your menstrual cycle. For example, if you ate pizza last night, you would probably see the scale rise considerably this morning, primarily because the high sodium content of pizza holds water in your body for a while. But this would not be an accurate estimate of your weight gain or losses.

3. The scale can be dangerous psychologically. If you get up in the morning, get on the scale and see you've gained two pounds after

exercising hard and eating sensibly for a week, you feel discouraged and figure you may as well eat anyway. If you get on the scale and see you've lost two pounds, you feel you deserve a reward. In either case, the scale has prompted you to eat.

4. The scale can also be damaging by encouraging you to think of yourself as a "good" or "bad" person, depending on what the almighty numbers say. If the scale shows you've lost weight, you feel successful, powerful, and in control. If it is up, you feel defeated and out of control. Your self-esteem should never be tied to numbers on a scale.

What would you do if you didn't weigh yourself? Try on your favorite pair of jeans! Denim tends to be an unforgiving fabric. Pay attention to how those favorite jeans fit on occasion, and you will have the best feedback tool there is!

Clearly, the old information about dieting is outdated. While certain people may need to lose weight at certain times in their lives, for the majority of women dieting is an inappropriate means to an impossible dream.

The key is to eat a wide variety of wholesome foods to build your calorie-burning processes and protect your health. You do not need another diet plan to do that. You cannot, and should not, exist on rabbit food. You do not need to depend on dietary supplements or liquid diet plans. Your grocery store contains everything you need: lean fish and chicken, low-fat or nonfat dairy products, fresh fruits and vegetables, grains and pastas. A great trick here is to shop only the outer perimeter of the grocery store, where the fresh foods are kept— such as bakery items, seafood, produce, and fresh dairy products. Venture into the inner aisles only once a month or so to pick up your staples, and you can avoid the high-fat foods and snacks, as well as decrease your grocery budget, by not buying impulse items.

What You Can Do Right Now

Dump dieting. As a symbol of your resolve, go get the scale out of your bathroom. Put on a comfortable pair of walking shoes and carry your scale down to a neighborhood dumpster and heave it in. Continue your walk to your local bookstore to reward yourself with a copy of the latest low-fat, high-carbohydrate cookbook and learn some exciting new menu ideas. You will then have taken a giant step down the road to loving the body you were born with.

Legalize Eating Again

Life itself is the proper binge.

—Julia Child

True confessions . . .

I've heard more than a few food confessions in my day, and the odds are you have, too. See if this one sounds pretty typical:

"I was so bad yesterday. I ate two doughnuts during my morning break, and I was so disgusted with myself that of course I skipped lunch. Then when I got home and opened the cupboard to decide what to cook for dinner, I ate three Twinkies, two handfuls of Fritos, and polished off a whole row of double-stuffs. After that major lapse, I felt too upset to cook, so I ordered pizza for the family—I had to order two to get the special. I ended up eating three slices of that on top of everything else I did wrong. As you can see, I'm a mess. No self-control at all!"

Are we "criminals" because of our food choices?

If you take the food out of that confession and concentrate on the levels of remorse and self-disgust, guess what? You'd think this lady had just robbed a bank or run down an elderly couple out for an afternoon stroll! It is not too farfetched to conclude that eating "bad" food has become the moral equivalent of committing a crime. Even those of you who are extremely forgiving of the failings of others are quick to assume the roles of judge, jury, and executioner when it comes to your own food choices.

Stop feeling so damn guilty!

If we are going to love the bodies we were born with, we've got to legalize eating again and stop feeling so damn guilty about what

43

goes in our mouths. Notice I did *not* unilaterally proclaim the need to stop feeling guilty altogether. Sometimes, guilt is appropriate. If, for example, your doctor has told you that you have high cholesterol and you continue to eat two eggs fried in bacon grease every morning, or you continue to eat chocolate candy bars three times a day after learning you have diabetes, you have real reasons to feel troubled.

What we need to work on is recognizing when guilt is appropriate and when it is not. Rather than letting food guilt overwhelm us, we need to listen to it, make peace with it, and try to understand what it means. Start by taking ten minutes to analyze your feelings about what you eat.

How do you feel about what you eat?

Food Guilt: A Self-Examination

1. I feel guilty when I eat . . . (list at least 5 foods)

_____

_____

_____

_____

_____

2. When I was a child, I was made to feel guilty about food if I . . .

_____

_____

_____

_____

continued

3. My favorite times to eat are when . . .

_____

_____

_____

_____

4. If I stopped feeling guilty about food and began to enjoy it, I'm afraid I would . . .

_____

_____

_____

5. Now, see if you can come up with one or two positive things that might result if you quit feeling so guilty about your food choices.

_____

_____

_____

As you worked your way through that exercise, did you see how you had been captured in the food-guilt trap? You didn't have any trouble at all coming up with five foods that made you feel guilty, did you? You probably could have named fifty foods without even pausing to think.

WHAT ABOUT FOOD GUILT IN YOUR CHILDHOOD?

Were you a member of the "clean your plate" club?

Most likely this one was easy for you, too. Millions of us were encouraged to clean our plates because of all the starving children in India or Africa. No one ever figured out how American kids eating all those dinners helped the starving kids one bit, but let's face it: most of us—at least those over a certain age—were made to feel guilty, wasteful, and unappreciative if we did not eat it all. Eating everything put in front of us made us "good" in someone's eyes.

This lesson often extends back into our childhood also. For many of us, the weekly visits to McDonald's or other fast-food restaurants considered commonplace now were unheard of when we were growing up. The rare visits to any type of restaurant were a cause for celebration of the liberation from one more tuna noodle casserole at home. This places dining out as a special treat and raises the ante psychologically when we're at parties or in a restaurant. "Well, I don't get this often, so therefore I am going to go for it! Laissez-faire, let the good times roll, and I'll pay for it later when I get home!"

Perhaps you also felt guilty if you ate more than your share of the good stuff. If you grew up as I did, with five voracious eaters for brothers, you probably learned that if the food was special, you better grab it straight from the grocery sack and start gobbling. Otherwise, you wouldn't get any. Later, when someone discovered the empty wrapper or wanted to know where the bag of chips went, you'd feign ignorance and feel guilty.

WHAT WERE YOUR FAVORITE TIMES TO EAT?

Do you eat "forbidden" foods when you're alone?

Did you pick occasions when you were all alone with your food? For busy women, *any* time alone can be a treat, but there's a good chance you're not really *enjoying* the "forbidden" foods you eat alone! If you find yourself sneaking away to eat alone furtively, where no one can see what you're doing, you have probably stored up a whole ton of food guilt. Pay close attention to every word in this chapter—getting rid of some of those guilt feelings is critical to your long-term success.

Did you pick social occasions when you were out with family or friends? It's easy to overeat when the party or event is the main attraction. Only later—on the way home or while getting into bed—do we think about the huge quantities of food we ate. The end result is often overwhelming guilt at not paying closer attention to what was going into our mouths.

Many of us growing up in large families also learned to "gobble" our food as a survival mechanism. If I turned my head at the table for one instant to grab the pepper, one of my brothers would have moved in for the "kill" on my food and attacked it with a fork! It would have been swallowed before I noticed it was gone. Those who ate the fastest simply got more food. Unfortunately for many of us, this lesson persists well into adulthood, long after the "plate snatchers" have moved on.

WHAT WERE SOME OF YOUR FEARS IF YOU LET THE GUILT GO?

Our relationship with food is almost religious.

Many of you are most afraid of *losing control*. You don't trust yourselves around food. This is partly because it has become invested with so much symbolism and moral power in America. Some social scientists believe this has happened because we have so little control over events in our neighborhoods, cities, and country that we want to exercise control over *something*. In any event, food has become a central sign of how well we can control ourselves. It's like a religious experience, only the final judgment of whether you are a good person or a bad one is based on food choices, not the old standbys like faith, hope, and charity.

Many more of you are most afraid of *getting fat*. You believe the old guilt syndrome is all that stands between you and obesity because it's what motivates you to "diet." Remember, though, that going on a "diet" is absolutely counterproductive, because every time you eat less, you encourage your body to store more fat.

Do you bury your feelings under a plate of food?

Some of the more honest among you will have admitted to being afraid of *facing your feelings*. Many times hunger has nothing to do with needing food. Stress, loneliness, fatigue, anger, disappointment, and boredom are just a few of the more common feelings that trigger eating and allow us to bury our feelings underneath the food. If we distract ourselves with food, we don't have to cope with those emotions.

For many women, food involves much more than hunger. It is deeply interwoven into memories of our past, our emotions on a day-to-day level, our feelings about ourselves, and our feelings about others. Because food is so intimately related to feelings for so many women, it is time to stop and think about whether you eat for reasons other than hunger.

Go through the following checklist and mark all those that apply to reasons you eat the foods you do. Even if you do only one of these on occasion, mark it anyway.

_____ Do you "make love" to your food?

Do you find comfort and solace in food? Does it provide reassurance and love that is nonconditional and doesn't hurt back?

_____ Are you a "procrastin-eater"?

Do you eat when faced with a big task that you would rather not do? Do you eat to avoid situations that need your attention?

_____ Are you a "make-'em-happy" eater?

Do you finish your plate at a dinner party because you don't want to offend your host or hostess? Or eat the special coffee cake your friend made because you successfully passed your twenty-ninth birthday nine times? Or eat those wonderful cookies your mom made especially for your visit?

_____ Are you an "anxiety" eater?

Do you eat in anticipation of that big interview on Monday? Or eat to calm your nerves about your impending divorce or other traumatic life event?

_____ Are you a "guilt" eater?

Do you eat because of unfulfilled expectations by yourself or others? Do you eat to heal wounds that only food can heal?

_____ Are you a "shame" eater?

Do you eat because you feel inadequate, out of sync with your body, yourself, or your actions? Do you eat over shameful events that may have happened years ago or just yesterday, leaving you feeling shamed and disgusted with yourself?

_____ Are you an "intimacy" eater?

Do you eat when you crave the closeness of someone else? Do you eat to fill a hole in the bottom of your stomach that only love from someone else could really fill? Do you eat to sate your unsatisfied sexual desires?

All of the above and probably some more of your own are reasons that many women eat. In a society that leaves many women feeling as if they have little or no control over their own lives, eating for emotional reasons is probably a given. Eating to cover feelings is only a symptom of a larger problem existing within both the individual and the greater social system we live in.

WERE YOU ABLE TO COME UP WITH ANY POSITIVE THINGS THAT MIGHT RESULT FROM ELIMINATING FOOD GUILT?

For many of you, the answer will be No. You have grown so used to feeling guilty about food that it's hard to envision anything positive coming out of letting that guilt go. Consider what might happen if you legalized eating:

Giving up some of your guilt feelings by legalizing eating again can ease your psychological need to atone for your food transgressions by dieting.

Good things happen when you let food-guilt go.

Remember, this country is full of people who wake up one morning and decide to give up red meat or some other food to make up for their "bad" choices of the day before. Sometimes they eliminate whole groups of foods without once considering the consequences on their bodies. They purchase mega-bottles of vitamins and minerals to replace the nutrients they are missing. They adopt the latest, most publicized diet on the market that week, and in the course of an hour or a day or a week or a month they abandon it for an eating binge—followed, of course, by a new diet. Without guilt as the driving force, you could be free of ridiculous diets and destructive eating habits forever.

Feeling guilty? Might as well eat some more.

Legalizing eating can rid you of a powerful negative emotion that often triggers eating. In spite of all the public-service messages stressing the importance of healthy eating, how do we appease the guilt we feel for making "bad" food choices? Too often, we do it with more of the same: "grab-bag" snack chips, pizzas the size of monsters' feet, and hamburgers big enough to satisfy a family of four's protein needs for the entire day.

No more saving calories for the healthy stuff.

Legalizing eating can help your health. Remember the confession at the beginning of this chapter? To make up for guilt over "bad" food choices, this woman did *without* all of the good foods her body needed for fuel and life functions: vegetables, fruits, and unprocessed grains were missing entirely! Give up the guilt and you no longer have to "save" calories for the foods your body needs.

Remember what real food tastes like?

Legalizing eating can free you to really enjoy food again. Do you even remember what real food tastes like? Fake flavors, chemical preservatives, and overprocessed mush are so common now that we have to make a real effort to enjoy our food.

How little we Americans actually enjoy our food was made profoundly clear to me when I spent a vacation biking through the French countryside. People *lived* to eat. The entire psychology of eating was different. These people approached their food with passion. Rich, voluptuous foods were heightened with flavors from fresh, fresh foods, available seasonally.

Why don't the French feel guilty? Where does all that passion for food come from?

Many of the foods were high in fat—more than a little unsettling to a dietitian! But the portions of high-fat foods were small, with lots of breads, fruits, and vegetables rounding out each meal. The flavors were so intense, varied, and profound that each bite was an experience in itself. All-you-can-eat specials did not exist.

Neither did obesity. Neither did guilt. These people had never heard of a stair-stepping machine or a TV tray. Instead of feeling one shred of guilt, they really "dined" at dinner. They lingered. They conversed. They drank (naturally!), they shared, they laughed, they communicated. When I arrived back home, I longed for the strong, rich flavors. I missed the camaraderie, the vitality, and the time the French devoted to eating. I grew an herb garden. I studied French cooking. I experimented with flavors and learned to linger over meals with friends and family members. I started to truly enjoy eating real food again.

Legalizing eating allows you to find your natural appetite again.

I might not get another chance, so I better order it now.

Have you ever been out for dinner, stuffed yourself silly, then groaned as the waiter passed the dessert tray right in front of your eyes? Did you order the mocha fudge cheesecake just because it looked *so good* and you didn't think you'd have another chance to try it any time soon?

When we diet, the natural regulating mechanisms in our appetites get so messed up that we end up eating lots of things we aren't the least bit hungry for. After a whole week of "good" eating, we often see a gooey dessert as a reward, so we talk ourselves into it even though we don't want it. We're out for dinner. We won't be back soon. We can diet tomorrow.

Once you legalize eating again, you'll be much more likely to stop when you're full. You know the dessert will be there next time, and you won't be on a diet then, either. Or, if you want it today, you can order a small meal, like soup and salad, and then enjoy the dessert.

When you pay attention to your appetite and real physical hungers, you can eat when your body needs food and stop when it's had enough. Your natural appetite is a wonderful guide to how much to eat.

Over the years I have had scores of workshop participants stand up and say, "Well, Monica, what about my friend Jane? She eats anything she wants, never diets, and she's thinner than a rail! Why can some people eat like that and just *never* gain weight?"

We've all known people like Jane. They eat heartily, appear to exercise rarely, and seem to stay thin as can be. Many people will attribute it to some type of mysterious metabolic disorder or a genetic trait, but often these aren't the reasons. These people *think* differently. These people consider food a legal source of energy for their body, nothing more and nothing less. Eating is legal for them because they have never thought about *not* eating.

Have you ever watched closely a thin person's eating habits over weeks or months and not just day-to-day? It is truly amazing. They eat when they are hungry (how interesting!), stop when they are full, and don't eat foods they don't love. Sounds foreign, doesn't it?

Consider the case of a chocolate chip cookie. Imagine that today I tell you that from this very moment on, you can *never,* ever have another one. No more. That's it. What do you suppose will happen? Stop for a moment, put yourself in this position, and think about it.

If you imagined obsession over chocolate chip cookies, you're absolutely right. Even if you didn't like them before, now that I have removed them from your list of available foods you would think of them nearly every waking moment. It is human nature. Watch children. Take away their television privileges sometime. "Mom, when can we watch TV? Mom ... Mom? Mo-o-o-o-o-oMMMMMMM!" It becomes paramount in their minds, even if they didn't normally watch much TV.

When we restrict foods in our daily diets, it may be successful for a short while, but eventually many people begin to crave those same forbidden foods. Think about the last diet you were on. How did you feel not being able to enjoy the foods others around you were having? Did those foods gain importance in your mind? Did they gain power? Elevating foods to these levels causes food to become more than just fuel for your body; it becomes omnipotent. Candy bars become a reward for good behavior; ice cream and mashed potatoes become comfort foods when we're down, and buttered popcorn becomes a treat when we go to the movies.

Thin people don't think this way. Watch them closely and you will see a different type of eating behavior altogether. They choose foods they love to eat and eat them with vigor, often not paying a whole lot of attention to when or even whether they eat. (Ever meet someone who just *forgets* to eat?) They eat what their body needs, when it needs it. They approach food entirely differently from people who have dieted often.

Imagine that you are in a fine restaurant and stuffed to the brim after a fabulous meal. But the waiter just happens to pass by with a beautiful tray of desserts. "Well, I better order it tonight, because the way I feel right now, I am going to have to diet tomorrow anyway!" The waiter delivers the order and, even though it doesn't taste quite as good as you thought, you finish every last bite because tomorrow is D-Day (Diet Day).

The thin person next to you may have eaten a large meal as well. But when the dessert tray comes, she may choose to pass on it. If she does order it and doesn't like the taste of it, she will most likely leave it on her plate. Leave it? Yes. Because tomorrow, she can eat the mocha fudge pie if she wishes. She's not in the diet mode of thinking, and so therefore knows that she can have it the next day or the next day if she wants it. It is the same food, but a very different approach based on a very different way of thinking.

As you drive home, you think to yourself, "You know, that Jane just eats anything she wants and doesn't gain a pound!" What you don't see is that Jane may go several meals before she feels truly hungry again. She may eat sparsely at her next meal or meals. Because food is not an issue for her, she doesn't have to spend her days obsessing about whether to diet today or not, whether this food or that is better for her, or whether she should exercise or not. She pays attention to her body, is closely connected with it, and gives it what it tells her she needs, whether that be sleep, food, play, or fluids.

I am going to challenge you to eat the chocolate chip cookie. Tomorrow morning, eat only the food that you love. "Oh no," you're saying, "she's off her rocker!" No, trust me and start trusting your body. So here is the scenario. You wake up, and you have the chocolate chip cookie, or a bag of them, for breakfast (or any food that you have not considered "legal" for years). Enjoy the cookies, revel in them, and taste every last morsel. At lunch, eat some more. But you absolutely stop when you are full. Not ten minutes later, but *immediately* when your stomach *begins* to feel satisfied. Remember that you can have more later if you wish, so the legal food now begins to lose its power over you. By supper, you begin to feel quite full of chocolate chip cookies, and so you choose a few, and maybe have another food you really enjoy.

Now it is the day after tomorrow. What do you feel like eating? This is a tough one. After years of abusing your body, you have probably forgotten how to pay attention to its messages and really listen to what it is telling you. Through the years of being a Registered Dietitian, I have often found myself eating foods simply because they are healthy and will balance my food groups that day. On the way, I found it easy to put on extra pounds because I was eating "should food" instead of foods my body really wanted. By paying close attention to your body and being aware of the messages it sends, you will learn to give it what it really needs. By lunch time tomorrow, you will probably be quite sick of the cookies and will prefer something else, assuming you pay close attention.

As an exercise for this, go now and stand in front of your refrigerator. While there, think to yourself, "What do I feel like eating? Something crunchy? Salty? Sweet? Am I thirsty? Am I hungry at all?" Mentally go through all the food you have in your refrigerator, and find out which one feels just right for you now, if any.

Many of you may be skeptical of this, because you have spent so many years denying your body certain foods because of judgments you've made about them. But once you allow your body to tell you what it needs, you will be amazed to find it wants all sorts of healthy foods. Two days of chocolate chip cookies and I guarantee you will truly enjoy a salad instead of *having* to eat it to lose weight. Your body will ask for fresh fruit, grains, milk, yogurt, crunchy carrots and, yes, on occasion, potato chips.

Feeding your body the foods it needs is one of the most important steps you can take to love the body you were born with. Once you decide that there are no more forbidden foods, and that all food is legal, you will gather energy and power both psychologically and physically from not denying yourself.

My husband is one of those people who can eat anything and not gain weight. For years friends and family said to him, "Just wait, you will gain weight just like the rest of us when you get married." Seventeen years later, he hasn't changed a pound since the day I met him. And can he eat! But by watching his habits closely, I have learned through the years that food is not an essential part of his life and has no power as it does for constant dieters. If he came home from work after a bad day and I offered him that chocolate chip cookie, he would look at me like I'm crazy! "I said I had a bad day, not that I was hungry!" He would not understand the relationship between food and comfort that so many women have today. Instead, he would probably jump on his bike and go for a twenty-mile bike ride, returning refreshed and much less stressed. He doesn't take the bike ride because he has to, but because he is closely tuned in to his body and knows that he needs to get out and feel the wind in his hair. When he is busy and involved with things in his life, he will rarely take the time to stop and have a full meal. But when he does, the whole table gets cleared.

Watch the thin people in your life closely and really pay attention to the way they eat. Ask them about why they do the things they do. You will be very surprised. Ask them why they have never had to diet. Their answers will be helpful in your process of learning how to legalize eating again for yourself.

Tonight during dinner, I want you to do a little exercise. Scoop up your portions on your plate in the size you normally would. In the middle of the meal, once you have finished half of your food, get up from the table and make a telephone call you owe someone. Talk to them for a minimum of five minutes if not longer, and return to the table. Look at your food. Are you still hungry? Pay attention to your level of hunger. What does your stomach feel like? You will most likely find that the amount of food you originally put on your plate is far more than you really needed, and certainly more than you will want when you return.

This is a real-life example of a mind-body connection. Most Americans eat their food so fast that the meal is over before the twenty minutes it takes to feel full from food. We shovel it in, not paying attention to how full the body is getting. Eventually, it becomes quite normal to eat past fullness and store up extra calories that add to extra weight gain.

Follow the Fist Rule.

If you don't yet trust your natural appetite, follow the Fist Rule. Make a fist, place it on a piece of paper, and trace around the outside of it. That is about how big your stomach is. Place your fist next to your midriff and look at it. That is how much food it takes to fill your stomach.

"No way. I'll be starving in an hour," you say. Perhaps you will. If you are, eat in an hour. Eat several times a day. Just keep the portions equivalent to your fist size.

Return to your favorite restaurant again. The bread basket is on the table, and you eat a couple of rolls while waiting for your salad. You eat your salad and realize you're full. When the entree finally arrives, you wonder how you'll ever eat it! Still, you paid for it, so you've got to get through it. Because the salad and rolls were about the size of your fist, you're full. While you waited for your entree, your hypothalamus gland let you know you could stop eating.

It's hard to get your fist's worth at all-you-can-eat specials!

Look at your fist one more time. Steak house meals, all-you-can-eat specials, fast-food combos—your body and your mind are not working together at all, are they? When you eat more than your fist's worth, you're not eating for hunger. Excuses like "I paid for it," "Mom's food is so good," and "Parties are just too fun" don't let you focus on your body's needs. Once you learn to trust your natural appetite and the fact that it's legal to eat again, you can let your body's natural appetite take over. In the meantime, try to follow the Fist Rule.

Legalizing eating can help you recapture the rich social side of food.

The good food/bad food dichotomies so prevalent in America have almost erased the rich social side of food. When we gather together to celebrate, we should linger in the moment. Even the simplest foods and tastes can seem rich in our mouths and in our memories without tasting the least bit sinful when they are shared with others.

Communal eating—what a fun way to enjoy food again!

A lot of the guilt we feel about food hides an even deeper hunger for meaning in our lives. While we'll address that hunger later, right now you need to let the guilt surrounding food go. Free yourself to enjoy your community picnic or block party. Feast at Thanksgiving. Taste a little of everything, then compliment the cooks at your church potluck or family reunion. Invite friends over and serve them your most flavorful recipes. Spend the entire evening at the table in guilt-free enjoyment of the moment.

All of the food-guilt messages connected with not feeling slender enough or making pure enough food choices belong in the garbage can. All of the food-guilt messages designed to tempt you to try another diet or buy another product belong in the garbage can, too. No longer consider yourself a slave to food guilt but rather your body's friend—someone who knows the importance of eating plenty of healthy, nutritious foods to show her love for the body she was born with.

What You Can Do Right Now

1. Try to make sure that at least 75 percent of your food choices are healthy. Refuse to feel guilty because your percentage is not 100.
2. Spend more time lingering over your meals. Add rich discussions to your dinner table. Share your eating times with family and friends. Regain the kinship inherent in communal eating.
3. Savor food. Choose strong, vibrant flavors that are *fresh* and announce to your palate that they have arrived. Quit eating bland, heavily processed foods that give you no joy and never really satisfy you.
4. Reflect on the food-hunger connection. Understand that food can't fulfill the other kinds of hunger you experience in your life.

Reconnect Your Body and Mind

At every moment, our bodies are continually responding to the messages from our minds. So what messages is your mind giving your body?

—MARGO ADAIR

For a few minutes every morning, you stand in front of the mirror over your bathroom sink. You brush your teeth, fix your hair, and apply your makeup. Your body and your mind are so accustomed to this routine that they work in perfect harmony. Even a bad-hair day or clumpy mascara can't totally derail the connection. Your fingers and hands and arms still do exactly what your mind tells them to do. From the neck up, you look pretty much the way your mind expects you to look.

Remember clown mouth?

Now think back to when you first started wearing makeup. You eagerly rolled on that lipstick, but your fingers couldn't keep it inside your lip lines—you probably wound up with a good case of clown mouth. It took some practice to get where you are now.

But what about from the neck down? If you are like most women, you have taken a big psychological step away from the rest of your body. You see it as somehow separate from your head and your mind. Too often, your body is your antagonist—a foreign object that just won't cooperate with how you want it to look and act—like a lemon from the used car lot. Obviously, you'd have traded it in for a new model years ago if you'd had any say in the matter.

58

It's time for a major tuneup!

Since you don't, it's time to start polishing up "the old girl" and giving her the mental equivalent of a major tuneup. In recent years we have taken great leaps forward when it comes to understanding what powerful influences our minds can have on our bodies. Much of this newer research suggests that the mind and body can work together to heal illness, delay disease, improve overall health, and reduce stress. Our minds are powerful engines whose powers we have yet to tap fully. Still, we know enough to know that we *need* the resources that are ours when our bodies and minds work together.

"Parts" are only "parts."

Unfortunately, it is becoming easier and easier for us to disconnect emotionally and intellectually from our bodies. Advertising again plays a role in fostering this split by featuring perfect body parts—a rippled torso and abdomen in a NordicTrack ad, a perfect hand in a jewelry commercial, well-turned calves in a TV spot for walking pumps. The logical mental jump is to assume these bodies are completely perfect, that the faces and hair are also beautiful, that the fannies don't sag.

This emphasis on body parts subtly encourages us to think of our own bodies as separate pieces, too. But instead of focusing on the best parts, the way they do in commercials, we tend to emphasize the one or two parts we detest most:

When it comes to our bodies, we tend to see only the worst.

"Oh, my breasts sag. Just call me banana boobs."
"My hips are like battleships."
"I hate these thunder thighs."

I even knew one elderly lady who went to her grave obsessed with a "bad" body part. Before she died, she made her daughter-in-law promise to bury her in a high-necked blouse arranged to hide her double chin!

Often we forget that our bodies have purpose beyond appearance. Those "banana boobs" were created not for sexual exploitation but for feeding a newborn baby. Those "battleship hips" were meant not to burst through doors but to provide a skeletal "carriage" for the growing fetus. Those hated "thunder thighs" were designed not for gimmicky toning machines but to provide the ideal repository for the extra calories needed to support the long months of pregnancy.

Focusing on one negative part of your body exacerbates your mind-body split. You need your body and mind to work together harmoniously all day long, just as they do for those few minutes in the morning. Most of your body parts are wonderful. Together, they make you a complete woman.

To reconnect your body and your mind and unleash all that stored-up power, you need to shift your focus from the negative to the positive. Put the spotlight on the things about you that make you an excellent person.

Are you great with kids? Do you let the little worries in life roll off your shoulders? Think of what is really great about you!

I May Not Be Perfect, But Parts of Me Are Excellent!

Identify ten things about yourself that you love. You can start with the ones you identified during your Body Image Assessment back in Step One, then add to the list. Do *not* be modest.

Do you have beautiful, thick hair? Fantastic color?
Do you have a great sense of humor? Can you laugh easily?
Are you committed to a cause? Do you stand by your beliefs?
Do you have strong money skills? Are you a budget whiz?

Write your list as quickly as you can. If, and only if, you have difficulty coming up with all ten, you can ask someone close to you for their help.

1. _____
2. _____
3. _____
4. _____
5. _____
6. _____
7. _____
8. _____
9. _____
10. _____

Listen to the language your body speaks.

Wasn't that fun? Parts of you are truly excellent! There is much more to the real you than a pile of broken pieces. You are a well-rounded woman with many positive character traits!

Focusing on your most positive parts is only one of the ways you can reconnect your body and your mind. Another is to tune in to the physical cues your body sends your mind. Have you ever tried listening—really listening—to what your body is saying?

To underline how easy it is to ignore even your body's loudest messages, look at a couple of extreme examples. The first involves a young woman with anorexia nervosa whose body was in the final stages of deterioration, yet she routinely worked out at the gym for several hours a day. She had effectively shut down all communication between her mind and body—the fact that she belonged in a hospital bed did not stop her from exercising at high intensity and living on two bowls a day of Special K with skim milk. Even the fact that her heart along with tissues from her other vital organs were being used as fuel for those workouts had no impact. She was in what the rest of us call total denial.

Disconnecting your mind from your body can have disastrous results.

Perhaps the most bizarre mind-body split I ever encountered was in a young college student who dropped by my college health-service office one day. She was bulimic—so driven to consume vast quantities of food that she had used up all her student loan money on groceries early in the semester. Still, her insatiable urge to eat overruled everything else. For many weeks, she had been eating a large container of dry oatmeal every day. When that got too expensive, she resorted to a fifty-pound sack of dry dog food for her week's groceries. That was the only thing she could think of that would let her eat as much as she wanted to eat cheaply and thus fill the empty void in her soul. Her mind was totally closed to the messages her body had to be sending it!

Drastic? Disgusting? Of course! But many of us find it hard to respond to our bodies' physical cues concerning food. We snack when we're not hungry, keep eating long after we're full, and routinely consume things we know are not good for our bodies.

Can you tell when your body is telling you it is thirsty, tired, stressed, or hungry? Think about some of the many ways your body tries to communicate with your mind.

*Stop and spend
some time
listening to your
body's messages.*

How Do You Read the Messages Your Body Sends?

Listed below are some of the common messages your body sends
to your mind. Sometimes you ignore these messages, and sometimes you pay attention to them. For example, if you keep yawn-
ing, you may ignore the message that you are sleepy and agree to
go shopping with your friend. Another time, you may listen to
your body and just go to bed. Write down how your mind reads
the signals your body sends you for each of its needs listed below.
Then think of one or two ways you have ignored and/or acted on
these messages.

1. Thirst _____

    Ignore: _____

    Act: _____

2. Hunger _____

    Ignore: _____

    Act: _____

3. Stress _____

    Ignore: _____

    Act: _____

4. Fatigue _____

    Ignore: _____

    Act: _____

5. Anger _____

    Ignore: _____

    Act: _____

continued

6. Nervousness _____

    Ignore: _____

    Act: _____

7. Sexual Desire _____

    Ignore: _____

    Act: _____

The dangers of ignoring our bodies' messages.

Now let's look specifically at some of the ways we ignore the messages our bodies send us about the food we are eating.

Do you remember how we talked in the last chapter about "good" and "bad" foods and the danger of investing what we eat with moral power? When we label foods this way with our minds, we instantly cut off the natural flow of information from our bodies.

For example, you may think ice cream is bad for you. You make this judgment in your head because you know ice cream has a lot of fat calories. But if you reached this mental conclusion without any input from your body, it's sort of like deciding it's cold outside because someone said so, not because you stepped outside and checked.

How does food really make you feel?

By not putting mental judgments on your food, you can allow your body to send you messages. Maybe you'll get an "ice cream headache" or your teeth will hurt, but you will definitely know how the ice cream makes you feel. Maybe a little tastes great, but a lot makes you feel sick.

By listening to your body's feedback, you can be open and attentive to your food. Then you can begin to make connections between what you eat and how it makes you feel. This feedback will teach you more about your individual needs than any book could begin to! If a particular food makes you queasy, you can choose not to eat that food again (at least not in that amount!).

For instance, I no longer order a Big Mac if I take my kids to McDonald's. Many people ask me how I can stand it, but it's very simple. One day I paid close attention to how my body felt after I had eaten a Big Mac. I felt sluggish. I was thirsty from all the salt. My stomach felt bloated. I didn't like those feelings, so now I choose to pass on the Big Macs and other high-fat foods. I do not feel deprived—I feel better!

Listen to the feedback your body gives you.

For the next twenty-four hours, pay close attention to how the food you eat makes you feel. Try to let your body give you as much feedback as possible. Concentrate on listening to what it is telling you. Are you hungry again soon? Do you feel tired or cranky? Also consider why you ate that food in the first place. Was it something you love or was it just there? Were you hungry or bored? Use the One-Day Food Record to record everything you eat. Include the time you ate each food, how you felt up to an hour after eating it, and all the reasons you chose to eat what you did.

Pay particular attention to the way concentrated sugars (such as regular soda and candy) as well as highly concentrated fat foods (such as snack chips, bacon double cheeseburgers, and french fries) make you feel. These foods tend to have noticeable effects on your body that occur for some time after you eat them. Start to notice them!

A day in the life of...

One-Day Food Record

FOOD	TIME	FEELINGS AFTER EATING	REASONS FOR EATING

continued

FOOD	TIME	FEELINGS AFTER EATING	REASONS FOR EATING
____	____	_____	_____
____	____	_____	_____
____	____	_____	_____
____	____	_____	_____
____	____	_____	_____
____	____	_____	_____
____	____	_____	_____
____	____	_____	_____
____	____	_____	_____
____	____	_____	_____
____	____	_____	_____
____	____	_____	_____
____	____	_____	_____

Reflect on your day. What did you learn about your body from this experience? Could you hear the messages being sent to your mind? Did you notice any nonfood signals from your body that your mind was also choosing to ignore?

It wasn't that hard to reconnect your mind and your body when you really worked at it, was it? To strengthen this new relationship, write your body a letter. Thank your body for all the things you have asked it to do for you—work hard, exercise, diet, skip sleep. Also apologize to it for all the wear and tear it has suffered. Try to put into words how you have treated your body for the last few years and how you now feel about what you have done.

It's time to say thanks.

Dear Body,

_____

_____

_____

_____

_____

_____

_____

_____

_____

_____

_____

_____

_____

_____

_____

_____

_____

_____

_____

_____

_____

_____

_____

_____

_____

_____

_____

_____

_____

Now try to capture how your body has been feeling all these years. Be your body and write your mind a letter. Share your feelings about how it has felt to be mistreated and ignored—thought of as an object worthy of scorn rather than as a vital part of the total *you*. Then thank your mind for the good things it has done for you:

Your mind has done lots of wonderful things for you.

Dear Mind,

_____

_____

_____

_____

_____

_____

_____

_____

_____

_____

_____

_____

_____

_____

_____

_____

_____

_____

_____

_____

_____

_____

Spend some quality time together.

Can you feel your body and mind gradually getting reacquainted? You have already taken several positive steps toward establishing a permanent connection, but now you need to spend some quality time together—just as you would with an old friend. This may seem like a hilarious suggestion, but it will take time for your body and mind to truly know each other.

One of the best ways to use your time together is to reacquaint yourself with the ways your body moves, responds, works, and feels. Activities like stretching, dancing, and yoga require a conscious effort from your mind to move your body into position, so they are all excellent ways to forge your reconnection.

Pay close attention to the way your body moves.

For example, if you are seated on the floor, legs outstretched, and you are attempting to touch your toes or ankles (for some of us inflexible types, the knees!), you can feel your muscles working and pulling. To fully stretch, you must send a mental message to go a little farther. As long as you're down there, hold your calves in your hands. Feel how the muscles stretch and pull to obey your commands? Consciously notice your knees' bony structure, and think of all the work they do for you each day. Grab your thighs. Think about the power there in these large, strong muscles. When you do this kind of movement exercise, you send your body messages on alignment and posture, forcing your body and mind to connect.

Aerobic activities like running, walking, rollerblading, and biking require a different kind of concentration, centered on moving you onward. While they are great for getting you fit, they are not substitutes for the more mentally demanding activities that actively encourage your body and mind to work together.

The activities below are all excellent ways to give your body a chance to reconnect with your mind. Circle the activities that you think you might enjoy:

1. Stretching	5. Pilates exercises
2. Weight lifting	6. Calisthenics
3. Dancing	7. Martial arts
4. Yoga	8. Callanetics

Spend time with your body each day.

Now circle a time of day that you could set aside for getting reacquainted with your body—just the way you set aside time for your face and hair!

1. Early morning, as soon as I wake up
2. Morning, after the kids leave for school
3. At work, when I need a break from my desk
4. At night, right before bed
5. Other_____

Look at your circled responses and think of them as goals. Commit yourself to spending a few minutes each day focusing on how your body moves, feels, and responds to your demands. When you do your movement exercises, feel the muscles pull and stretch. Feel the parts that are flexible and the ones that need more work.

Learn to recognize your body's cues.

Genuine movements of the body can result in genuine connections with the mind. Once your body and mind are used to working together, you will find it much easier to recognize the cues your body gives you regarding hunger, sleep, thirst, stress, and its need to move.

What You Can Do Right Now

1. Commit yourself to spending a few minutes a day learning about your body again and celebrating your physical being.
2. Shut the blinds, put on some music, and dance to the rhythm your mind hears and your body feels. Welcome home, stranger!

Say Good-bye to Hurtful Shame

Creative minds have always been known to survive any kind of bad training.

—ANNA FREUD

Congratulations! You just hit the halfway mark.

It's time to stand up, walk around, shake your shoulders, and take the equivalent of baseball's "seventh-inning" stretch. You have just completed the first half of your workbook! Some of you formerly compulsive dieters have probably been working on this nonstop—with the same zeal you used to reserve for your latest dieting effort!

So, before we go on, take a few minutes to look back at how far you've traveled down the road to loving the body you were born with:

- You took an honest, naked (!) look at your body and realized that many of your "imperfections" were genetic.
- You saw how you had been manipulated into believing thin equaled beautiful even though only 2 percent of the population can ever achieve that "ideal."
- You vowed to quit hurting your body by dieting and counting calories and making it think it had to store fat to save your life. You even tossed your bathroom scales in the garbage! (If you didn't, go do it right now.)
- You realized food does *not* have the moral power to make you good or bad, and you do *not* need to feel guilty about your food choices.

- You plugged in the internal connection joining your body and your mind and started really listening to your body's messages.

Is your body feeling like your friend?

In other words, you have run and walked and crawled the mental equivalent of a few marathons! You are beginning to accept yourself for who and what *you* are. And even if you don't trust it completely yet, you have finally begun to make friends with your body. You are developing what social scientists call a "healthy" body image.

Shame can be a heavy burden.

For many of you, there is still one gigantic obstacle standing between you and success. That obstacle is shame. If you are carrying around a duffel bag full of destructive shame, you already know it only grows heavier with time. Working through the exercises in this chapter can give you the courage to put it down and move on with your life.

Women who have suffered through sexual abuse or other shaming of their bodies often have difficulty loving their bodies and enjoying sexual pleasure, because they were betrayed. Since that time, their perception of pleasure has become marred by all the excess baggage that is involved in the loss of feeling one's body as a sacred and private sanctuary. They often fear too much pleasure because they don't believe they deserve it. Some women feel betrayed by their own bodies.

If this describes you, it is time to start turning this thinking around. It is not that our bodies betrayed us, but that our bodies were betrayed!

Shame can become strong enough in some women that they begin to believe they are bad or inferior in many respects. *There is something wrong with me. I am inadequate. If others find out, I will be alone and abandoned. Everyone will see through me and know that I am really worthless.*

Shame is not always harmful. Shame helps us to recognize that we are human and that we have limits. Shame serves to remind us that we are not perfect and the master of all. Shame can act as a tool to allow us to accept our mistakes; it gives us a chance to fix them. Shame also serves to encourage us to develop a set of social skills and parameters that give us a sense of competence, and it allows us to understand what is acceptable by the larger group.

Think about the pat phrase many children hear growing up:

"Shame on you!" This phrase is used to remind children that they are stepping out of their boundaries with their behavior and outside the realm of adult expectations. Children raised with a clear sense of values do not need to be reminded that they have committed a shameful event. Instead, discussing with children the inappropriateness of their behavior and its reasons will result in a deeper understanding and longer lasting change for the child than the harshness of the single comment, "Shame on you!"

All too often, parents use shame in regard to eating habits or weight and physical features. Children are shamed for not cleaning their plate of food, for not fitting the ideal image the parent has regarding their size or weight, for eating what the parent deems is "too much" when the child is already "pudgy," and so forth. Shame of this nature harms the growing child and helps to establish early that eating and our bodies are a source of shame, particularly for females.

Although shame can come from deeply emotional and traumatic events in our lives, shame can also come from seemingly innocuous sources. The majority of my clients with negative body image began their search for the perfect body after a single, seemingly innocent, remark by another person, most often someone important to them. A brother's chiding on the fatness of your thighs, an uncle's flippant remark about your blossoming body, or your father's offhand comment concerning your breast size can be all it takes for some young women to begin the pursuit of the perfect body.

Although young girls typically hold the men in their life in high esteem, men are not the only culprits. In the early seventies, bright-colored patches all over clothes were the rage. Being a teen, I wanted to fit in, and so I had patched a hole in the seat of my jeans with a bright rainbow patch. My grandmother was aghast! She told my mother in front of me that I looked like a "whore" and that I was advertising my body by drawing attention to my buttocks. I felt horribly shamed, and never wore those jeans again. Yet even worse, I was never able to forget the searing pain that comment made me feel, and I never felt as close to that grandmother again.

It is difficult to imagine the extent of harm that these types of comments can do to a young woman who is already suffering fears about her changing body and searching for her own identity in the maze of adolescence. I plead with my audiences, especially the men, to *never, ever* comment about anything remotely close to the young girl's body. Although this can be especially detrimental during the teen years, it can have negative effects throughout the childhood years.

The father of a four-year-old girl called in to a talk show I was appearing on and asked what he might do to curb his daughter's need to stand in front of the mirror and criticize her body. As it turned out, the father often commented about how beautiful his baby was (focusing on her appearance), and her mother was a lifelong chronic dieter. Growing up watching a mother who is self-critical of her body and constantly pursuing the latest diet fads can affect young girls negatively also. *How can I be happy with my body when the mother I came from is so disgusted with hers?*

As we have seen, shame can be a harmful, powerful, and destructive emotion that may stem from many different sources and can stand in the way of loving our bodies the way we need to. Shame over our past histories can contribute to addictions and can do considerable damage to our bodies, minds, and spirits. Filled with shame and self-loathing, women often feel justified in turning their buried anger and hurt inward and harming their most wonderful and powerful bodies. It is time for you now to think about shame in your life and where it may have come from.

Recall a Shameful Experience

Begin by thinking of a time in your life when you felt deeply ashamed. Stop for a few minutes. Close your eyes. Bring the shameful or embarrassing moment to the front of your memory. As you replay the scene, what do you feel?

- A flushed face?
- A sick feeling in your stomach?
- Sweaty palms?
- A shiver down your spine?

Begin to understand this complicated human emotion.

Sometimes, these memories hurt so much that you have a strong need to turn away from the images. This is because shame is a painful, complicated human emotion. It can be difficult even to give words to the actual feelings. Our language seems so inadequate when it comes to describing something this complex.

Keep in mind that shame varies from one individual to another. What you may find horribly shameful may be only slightly embarrassing to someone else. In fact, shame includes a lot of emotions known by other names: embarrassment, humiliation, disgrace, dishonor, even self-consciousness.

Identify the sources.

Shame can stem from many experiences in a woman's life. As you look at the list of some of the most common sources connected to your body, identify those areas of your life where shame may have become part of your experience.

Shame: Identifying the Sources

_____ Childhood sexual abuse
Were you touched in a shameful way or sexually molested?

_____ Masturbation
Were you taught that masturbation was wrong? Did anyone say you could go blind or grow hair on your palms?

_____ Rape, including attempted rape and acquaintance rape
Were you made to feel sexually shamed by a stranger or by someone you knew and trusted?

_____ Abortion
Have you felt shame about this decision?

_____ Sex that doesn't fit "typical" norms, like homosexual or "forbidden" sexual experiences
Have you felt shame over experimentation?

continued

_____ Extramarital sex or secret relationships
Have you felt shamed for being disloyal?

_____ Sexually transmitted diseases
Have you felt shamed for carrying diseases only "others" get?

_____ Sexual harassment
Have you felt shame over unwanted advances?

_____ Normal stages of life
Did you feel shame as parts of your body changed—getting your first menstrual cycle, watching your breasts grow, finding you had stretch marks?

_____ Passing comments by others
Did you feel shamed by a glib comment someone made regarding the way your body looked or about your weight or shape?

What is shame to one might well be anger or another emotion to someone else.

None of the experiences in the list automatically means you feel shame. Each of us has individual experiences and histories that determine how we will react when it comes to our bodies. For example, I have known women who had had abortions and felt only a little sadness, while others were consumed with guilt and shame.

I have known women who felt extreme anger—even rage—at the person who infected them with a sexually transmitted disease, while others felt mainly despair and shame. Most health professionals consider masturbation perfectly normal, and many women feel satisfaction as their primary emotion after masturbating. Others who grew up in an environment where it was considered "dirty" or sinful might feel only self-disgust and shame.

If *you* feel shame about something, then it doesn't really matter how anyone else might feel in the same situation. All that matters is what it is doing to your life.

Does it still have power over you?

Go Back to Your Shameful Experience

Recall once more that time in your life when you felt deeply ashamed. This time, try to think through the details so that you can experience how your body feels about this shame.

1. What exactly was shameful about it?

_____

_____

2. Where did you learn that this was a shameful experience?

_____

_____

3. Who was (or may have been) hurt by it?

_____

_____

4. What price have you paid for this shame regarding the way you feel about your body?

_____

_____

5. Does this shame still have power over you?

_____

For some women, shame over past experiences is so profound that it inhibits their ability to function as normal, healthy adults. This is especially true of women who have been sexually abused, and it is now thought that one in four women has experienced some type of sexual abuse!

Through most of civilization and in most cultures, sexual abuse has been a deep secret. People denied its existence, and those who insisted on revealing the truth about it were thought to be telling stories. Finally, this last taboo has been broken, and women need not suffer the burdens of sexual abuse anymore. Although that doesn't make the process of discussing it much easier for women, it does provide resources and avenues that allow us to share this burden with others and begin to heal the wounds.

The first time "Julie" came to my office, she appeared to be a bright, spirited young woman. She bantered on through our initial conversation, sharing with me her passion for gymnastics and college. Only on later visits, as we got to know each other better, did she begin to share her innermost dark secrets of daily vomiting of the minuscule amounts of food she did eat. She was taking laxatives several times a day, to the point they were interfering with her ability to attend classes. Although all medical tests came back indicating no other health problems, she suffered from constant fatigue and difficulty completing her required three hours of daily gymnastics practice. Julie saw herself as a total failure. Despite her successes as one of the most important women on the team and her excellent grades, she felt that all those she met saw her for the impostor she felt she really was. As time wore on, Julie's history of sexual abuse as a child surfaced in her counseling sessions. She had no interest in dating in college, and had no intimate relationships, due in part to the shame she felt over her father's sexual abuse of her. She suffered from intense self-shame internally, and had transferred that shame to her body when a coach she held in high regard had commented negatively about her weight one day. It took almost three years and intensive counseling with a therapist and myself before she began to regain the essential core of self-esteem that stopped her from abusing her body so rigidly.

Diffuse some of the shame's power.

If you are included in this group of women who have been sexually abused, you might already have worked through your shame by going to counseling or receiving open support from family and friends. If you have retained it inside, as many women do, there is a very real danger that the shame has grown to immense proportions and spilled over into other areas of your life. Speaking with someone else in a trusted, safe situation can diffuse some of the shame's power. The person you talk to can be a therapist or a minister or even a close friend you trust implicitly, but sharing and talking through the experience is critical—shame gains its power primarily because the experience is so secretive.

Find a quiet place to reflect on your past. Can you think of any other shameful experiences? Try to describe them:

_____

_____

_____

How have these experiences gained power over the way you feel about your body?

_____

_____

_____

_____

_____

How have you been victimized by your shame?

_____

_____

Do you have someone in your life you could share this shame with? Who?

_____

How do you think this person would respond?

_____

_____

One of the greatest tragedies of shame is that it can rear its ugly head in the vital connections between our mind and body. Shame can dull our senses and not allow us to see, touch, and feel the world as it truly is. Feelings of being betrayed will not allow us to enjoy the splendor of our own sexuality and revel in its richness and source of pleasure. In the next chapter we will work toward restoring the relationships you have with your sensuality and sexuality, a vital step in learning to love the body you were born with.

You do not need to carry this alone.

Remember, shame has enormous destructive powers when it comes to the ways women live their lives and feel about their bodies, especially if it is kept hidden. Sharing the shame with others helps dismantle its power. We are all human. We all have imperfections. You do not need to carry this huge burden alone. It will take courage, but you can put it down and refuse to let shame sabotage your efforts to love and enjoy your body.

What You Can Do Right Now

Put down your pen and begin to relax. Breathe slowly through your nose and exhale through your mouth. Find a comfortable position and feel your muscles relax. Focus on a positive thought or experience you have had. Now, slowly, begin to imagine yourself with no shame. Feel a sense of letting go as all the shame you can remember flows out of your body. Let it go. There are no hurtful, "bad" things about your body—only good. Your body is free of the chains that have bound you. You are comfortable within your body. You can feel its strength and power. Tell your body how wonderful it feels to be comfortable with it again. Think how much better your life will be without shameful thoughts infecting your relationship with your body.

Make an appointment for an hour with a masseuse. Nothing else is quite as nourishing to your healthy sense of self and touch.

Reawaken Your Senses

Each day, and the living of it, has to be a conscious creation in which discipline and order are relieved with some play and pure foolishness.

—MAY SARTON

I'm suggesting we call sex something else, and it should include everything from kissing to sitting close together.

—SHERE HITE

It's time for some fine-tuning.

When you plugged in the internal connection joining your body and your mind, you *felt* the music in your body and *heard* it in your head. For many of us, this reconnection of body and mind is like getting a new power supply for an old stereo. Once we make the initial connection and get on the right wavelength, we can feel and hear our body's messages coming through loud and clear.

As we learn to rid ourselves of the hurtful shame we worked on in the last chapter, we can begin to pay attention to the music instead of the annoying static. Initially, we may be just plain delighted to hear anything besides static and faded rumblings, but before long we're ready for some fine tuning.

Focusing on your senses is just that—fine-tuning the newly established connection between body and mind by strengthening the neural pathways that run between them. Experiment with how to best blend

81

the sounds and adjust the pitch, and you'll learn how to tune in to your sensual, sexual self. The endless variations you discover will provide music for your soul!

One of the most devastating repercussions of being shamed about our bodies is that it diminishes our enjoyment of sexuality. As we heal the scars that shame has made us feel about ourselves and our bodies, we can begin to truly enjoy and delight in our sexual desires and nurture our sensuality.

Loving the body you have is essential to healthy sexuality.

As you begin to explore and understand your sensual and sexual feelings, keep in mind that the line between the two is very blurred. Both involve physical sensations like seeing, touching, smelling, hearing, and tasting. In addition, your attitude toward both is shaped by many factors, including your background, your mood on any given day, your social situation, and your relationships. Once all the variables are taken into account, about the only universal conclusion that can be reached is that a healthy body image and an open attitude toward sensuality are essential components of healthy sexuality.

You have already made great progress toward establishing a healthy body image. Your body, once perceived as your enemy and nemesis, is gradually becoming your friend—an integral, vital part of your whole being. Like a friend, it can give you much pleasure. Later in this chapter, you'll learn new ways to awaken your senses and heighten your sensuality, strengthening the bond between your body and mind even more.

What Is Sexuality?

For women, sexuality is a whole-body experience.

Before focusing on specific sensual experiences, let's first look at sexuality in general. As a concept, sexuality usually carries far more connotations for women than it does for men. For us, sexuality is a total-body, total-life experience—not just the act of intercourse. The sex act, in and of itself, cannot begin to define our feelings about our sexuality.

One of my close friends tells a story that illustrates this concept perfectly. She fell in love while she was still in high school, a few years before the widespread availability of effective contraceptives gave rise to the sexual revolution of the 1960s. The fear of pregnancy was still very real, so this couple always managed to stop themselves just short of intercourse.

When's the last time you steamed up your car windows?

"The car windows would be steamed over for hours while we did everything but! I was madly in love and felt like a real sexual animal, but when we finally got married, sex was a major disappointment. Instead of hours of kissing and touching and holding and holding back, it was just slam, bam, thank-you ma'am. We were married for years before we finally learned how to recapture what we'd had in the back seat of that old Chevy."

What they'd had, of course, were hours of sexuality without the actual sex, heightened by the kind of hot romance that involves *all* of the senses. When the genital-centered sex act became the primary focus, much of the sexuality was lost—particularly from the female perspective.

A woman's whole body and being can be sexual! In recent years, as more and more women have identified and described their attitudes and feelings about sexuality based on their own experiences and feelings, we are finally getting a realistic view of female sexuality. Traditional definitions and views of sexuality were rooted in this country's puritanical foundations, when the body was thought to be a work tool, and are by their very nature outdated and limiting. Physical pleasures back then were considered sinful. Even modern dictionaries describe the negative connotations of sexuality, citing an "excessive" interest in sex as one of the main definitions of the term, along with "sexual activity" and "the condition of having sex."

We've been typecast as madonnas or whores.

In that context, it is not surprising that women have traditionally been represented as either madonnas or whores. The madonna is virtually asexual—she is the passive, submissive, dependent receptacle of a man's sexual desire and finds fulfillment in being the mother of his children. The opposing image is the whore—the tempting seductress who can overpower men with her wiles.

Although we know full well these images are seriously outdated and flawed, they continue to be perpetuated. Watch any soap opera or commercial that relies on sex to sell, and you'll still be inundated with images of scantily dressed whore-women, long hair blowing in the wind, attending parties and running off to their careers. In direct

How did we get stuck with the male definition of sexuality?

The times they are a-changin'.

opposition, you'll see the madonna women tending sick children late at night, scrubbing the kitchen floor in lovely clothes, and choosing the peanut butter only the best mothers buy.

Although these oppressive images were created by men, from a man's perspective, the most unfortunate part is that many women have been socialized to accept these outdated, irrational views of their sexuality.

Thanks in large part to both the women's movement of the last twenty-five years and the availability of effective birth control, which took a lot of the fear out of sex for women, we are now developing much broader definitions of female sexuality. They may not have made it into the dictionaries yet, but we now know our sexuality is not just a response to men's sexuality. It has its own characteristics, and as the woman in the backseat of the Chevy would tell you, all of our senses work together to deepen the experience. It involves not only physical gratification but also a sense of who we are as women in the context of our own lives, relationships, and emotions.

One of the negative effects of not loving the body you were born with is the strong hold it can create on sexual relationships. One of my workshop participants put it this way: "I wonder how many women have stuck with their husbands or boyfriends because they were terrified of going under the covers with a new man?" When we don't feel comfortable with our bodies and our sexuality, how can we find happiness in our relationships? How can we find a partner who will treat us with the love and respect we deserve?

Take a few minutes to explore your definition of sexuality. The exercises on the next few pages will help you define what the concept means to you in the context of your own life.

How do you feel about the whole question of sex and sexuality?

My Definition of Sexuality

1. Who taught you about sex? Circle all that apply.

Teacher(s)	Mother	Father
Sister(s)	Brother(s)	Girlfriend(s)
Boyfriend	Book(s)	Spouse/mate

2. What messages did you receive about sex while you were growing up? Circle all that apply.

Sex was healthy.	Sex was bad, especially for girls.
Sex was natural.	Sex was something secret.
Sex was exciting.	Sex was only for married people.
Sex was "dirty."	Polite people didn't talk about sex.

Other (be specific)_____

_____

3. In what ways (if any) did religion influence your sexuality as you were growing up?

_____

_____

_____

4. What do you like most about sex? Circle all that apply.

Kissing	Cuddling	Manual stimulation
Intercourse	Oral sex	Touching
Giving my partner pleasure		My own orgasms
Trying new positions		Getting it over with

Other_____

continued

5. What do you like least about sex? Circle all that apply.

Kissing   Cuddling   Manual stimulation
Intercourse   Oral sex   Touching
Giving my partner pleasure   Feeling I've been used
Trying new positions   Not being able to climax
Other_____

6. Does anything create anxiety for you about sex? If so, what?

_____

_____

7. Do you ever feel guilty about sex? If so, when?

_____

_____

8. When you think of past sexual relationships, which feelings are most typical for you? Circle all that apply.

Joy   Peacefulness   Confusion
Anger   Disgust   Anxiety
Shame   Hatred   Love
Satisfaction   Sorrow   Horror
Arousal   Embarrassment   Pride
Other_____

9. Why do you think you experience these feelings?

_____

_____

_____

continued

10. When you are having sex, how do you feel about your body?

_____

_____

_____

_____

_____

_____

_____

11. What does sexuality mean to you? Try to write your personal definition of this complex word.

_____

_____

_____

_____

_____

_____

12. Has your view of sexuality changed in the last ten years? If so, how?

_____

_____

_____

_____

_____

_____

Often, just writing down your feelings about your own sexuality can begin to clear away the baggage that gets in the way of experiencing a healthy sex life. Now that you have written yours here, I encourage you to come back and look at them from time to time. You will most likely be amazed at how your attitudes and feelings about sexuality change through time. Sexuality is one of the fundamental gifts of womanhood that ebbs and flows as one travels through the stages of life as a woman.

Sexuality and intimacy, although not the same, are often confused by many people. Although our sexuality refers to all that is sexual about us, intimacy is our ability to connect on a most basic level with another human being.

True intimacy does not have to be purely sexual. It is possible to have intimate relationships with others in our life, but only after having reconnected the body and mind and defined our own true spirit. Intimacy demands that there is a mutual level of respect, communication, and trust between two individuals, and until you present your true self, you will be unable to complete the picture. Because intimacy is such a vital part of a healthy sexual relationship, it is worthy of consideration as we learn to create our own definition of sexuality.

When is the last time you experienced true intimacy in your life?

For many women, this question usually evokes high-pitched, nervous laughter, most likely due to the anxiety this question prompts. Some women love intimacy yet rarely have the occasion to enjoy it, and still others have a difficult time with it because they *can't* experience it. You will be unable to connect intimately with others if you have not connected with yourself first. Your self is your spirit, the intuitive, feminine side of you. Without an understanding of your spirit, you are unable to participate fully in the act of sex or intimacy because you are presenting only a ghost of your true self to your partner. Your partner must resort to guessing who you really are, what your needs are, and what you are thinking, dreaming, or feeling. In my workshops over the years many men have expressed frustration and anger about this in the women they love. "How can I know what she needs when she won't tell me or when she just says, 'I'm fine?' I get tired and stop asking."

By reconnecting your body and mind, as well as working more on defining who you are as a unique individual, you will become one with yourself and your spirit. The sexual act will become an interchange of energy between the two of you because you are there in body *and* spirit. By being a whole person, confident and comfortable with your body and all that makes you who you are, you will be able to share your inner self with another and give energy as well as gain energy back from your partner.

In Praise of Your Feminine Nature

As I have discussed, the repeated promotion of thin women in the media has had detrimental effects on us. One of the more subtle but very powerful impacts of these images has been the disgust and disdain women have developed for their feminine nature. Although it is relatively easy to understand how women can learn to hate their thighs through constant exposure to these images, it is difficult to see the more subtle effects.

Douche ads tell us that our bodies are dirty and must be cleansed; deodorant ads tell us that our natural odors are a social trauma; and if we force our feet into stiletto high heels we will make our legs look lean and long. All of these messages serve to provide us with an external opinion of not only what is sexual, but also what is feminine—even if achieving these ideals comes with the risk of harming our bodies. Doctors warn us not to douche so as to not alter the chemistry of the vagina, that extended wearing of pantyhose creates a warm, moist breeding ground for yeast and bacterial infections, and that high heels can cause back problems; yet we persist in putting ourselves at risk.

Our feminine nature is complexly interwoven into our sexuality. By using external views of what is feminine and what is not, we have lost respect for the feminine sides of ourselves. In the process of disliking our bodies and attempting to change them, we have created a chasm that disconnects us from our feminine, sexual side. We cannot enjoy healthy sexuality, intimacy, or our sensual natures until we define for ourselves what being a woman really means to us.

What does your femininity mean to you?

_____

_____

_____

_____

How do you feel about being a woman? What do you like best? What do you like least?

_____

_____

_____

_____

Where did your views of what being a woman means come from?

_____

_____

_____

_____

Would you rather have been a male, or are you happy being a woman?

_____

_____

_____

_____

How did your mother influence your views of what it means to be feminine?

_____

_____

_____

_____

I grew up as the oldest and only daughter in a family of six children. My mother was a "matriarchal" woman, and I typically saw only her masculine side as she "ruled the roost" while my father was gone for long periods of time flying for the airlines. I always felt like one of the boys and grew up as the ultimate tomboy. Although this was a fantastic dress rehearsal for learning to deal with men in adult life, it left me unsure and out of touch with the wonderful feminine side of my nature. Only through nurturing the intuitive, feminine side of my personality was I able to grow into my own view of what it means to be a woman.

Developing our own unique ideas about sexuality and what the experience of being a woman is like for us as individuals is an important step in learning to love our feminine bodies. The next step is to look at other ways our culture can define our views about what sexuality means to us.

Some of the most damaging sexual scripts in our culture occur for young girls during adolescence. They grow up with a dualistic type of thinking. They learn that they can be victimized by sex, become pregnant, or get diseases. All of these fears are very real and a necessary evil of raising young women. But what about the young woman's natural desires? Rarely, if ever, is the topic of desire discussed with young girls in our culture.

Girls must always provide the "no" that cannot be expected of young, virile boys. For young men in our society, their sexual desire is an assumption that is taken for granted. Consider for a moment the charges and names the young girl accrues when she expresses her natural desires. "Slut," "whore," or "loose" are commonly heard, while young men expressing the same desires are "studly," "macho," or have "balls." Young girls grow up believing that their desire is somehow controllable and shameful, whereas sexual drives in boys are admirable.

These complicated feelings set the stage for the development of unhealthy sexual attitudes later in life, when the woman is confused and unsure how to read the messages her body is sending about sexual desire. It is no wonder that women grow up inattentive or ignorant of their sexual desires and never learn alternative methods of dealing with them outside the act of sexual intercourse. Allowing women to accept their sexual desires as a natural part of life would also allow them to find different methods of expressing these strong feelings. Remember the woman in the Chevy?

Unfortunately, in American society it is too often believed that if these natural desires are discussed, then they will be acted on as if the young girl has been given permission—even in a culture with the highest rate of teen pregnancy of any developed country in the world. Maybe it is time to start accepting sexual desire and discussing it with our young women as the natural part of a woman's life that it is.

Does your sexual script look like this?

Sexual Scripts

In our culture, men and women are assigned "sexual scripts." These are the thoughts, feelings, and myths that we grew up believing were true. The female sexual script often reads like this:

1. Sex is good for having babies and bad if it brings pleasure.
2. Sex is for men.
3. Men should know what women want.
4. Women should have sex but not talk about it.
5. Women should look like Playboy Playmates.
6. Women are nurturers.
7. Sex is a failure without an orgasm.

How mythical are these scripts? To what extent have they been incorporated into your own sexual script or those of your peers? How much may they have influenced your thinking?

_____
_____
_____
_____
_____

continued

Europeans have much different sexual scripts.

Should we share our feminine views about sex with other women? Try to rewrite our sexual scripts?

Sexual scripts written for American women differ greatly from those used in other cultures. In Europe, for instance, sex is openly discussed and considered an essential part of life. European women have much more positive attitudes about their bodies: they feel thoroughly comfortable in *their* bathing suits and often shed the tops. Ironically, their teen pregnancy rates are much lower than ours.

Our sexual scripts are outdated and tired, encouraging us to be secretive about sex. The media features unrealistic models, and because we don't usually share our feminine views about sex with other women, we tend to feel we can never measure up, further alienating our bodies from our sexual feelings.

What Is Sensuality?

Are you suffering from sensorial anorexia?

Men are more visual. Women are more emotional.

Every one of our senses plays a role in our sexuality. When we make love, we use them *all* to deepen the experience. Nurturing our senses and paying close attention to the many sensations our bodies enjoy can help us reconnect with our sexuality. This is especially important for women who have spent their entire adult lives on diets or been extremely concerned with their bodily imperfections.

The sensual differences between men and women are readily apparent during sex, where men rely more heavily on their visual sense than women do. Some researchers argue that pornography has contributed to this by presenting women as objects—the body (the visual image) is separate from the living, complex individual with a multitude of needs (the woman). Others speculate that men are more sensitive to light and shape because of their right-brain development, while females appear to be more sensitive to emotional characteristics associated with the left brain.

In any event, the visual aspect of sex does receive more emphasis than any other in our culture. Women are routinely displayed as ornamental objects. In a one-dimensional medium such as a magazine advertisement, the other senses are totally lost. This contributes to the mind-body split for many women, who often turn their backs on their sensual natures. Others simply don't have the time or energy to devote to nurturing the sensual sides of their being.

Tune in to your sensual symphony.

Over the next few pages, you will learn many different ways to get in touch with your senses. Even a few minutes here and there can help you tune in to the sensual symphony waiting to be played inside your body.

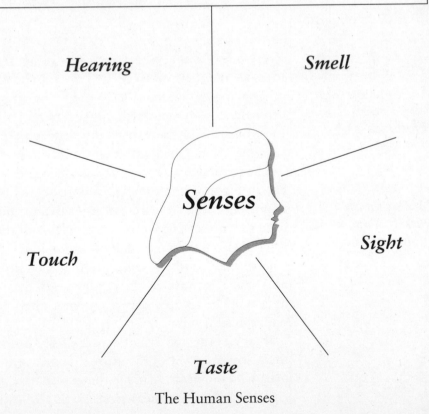

Ask Yourself . . .

1. Have I ever been treated like a sex "object"?
   By whom? How? Why?
2. What are some positive things I can do for myself so I don't feel "objectified" by sex?

Hearing

Smell

Senses

Touch

Sight

Taste

The Human Senses

TOUCHING

Touch connects us with others.

Touch is one of our most vital senses. It is probably the sense that is most obvious during sex, as touching often *seems* to be the sense that begins most sexual encounters. A friend's arm around us eases our sorrow, a spontaneous hug from a child warms our heart, the circle of hands in prayer lifts our spirit. Touch connects us with others in this human experience.

For many of us, though, touching is uncomfortable. It violates our private space. It can bring back memories of childhood shame or abuse. If our touch was once scorned, we may still be wearing the scars.

Take a few minutes to think about your relationship with touching. Start with your childhood. Do you remember the ways you were touched and allowed to touch others? Did you grow up in a high-touch or low-touch home?

_____

_____

_____

What does touch mean to you?

Was the touching in your childhood affectionate, or was it sometimes used for punishment as well?

_____

_____

_____

Has anyone in your life touched you so affectionately that you learned to trust your body? Try to describe those touches.

_____

_____

_____

continued

Have you ever been touched unwantedly or aggressively? How did this make you feel about your body?

_____

_____

_____

What kinds of touch give you the most pleasure in your sexual relationships? Circle all that apply.

Long, soft kisses   Gentle touches to all parts of body
Hugging   Cuddling and falling asleep together
Holding hands   Caressing of breasts and genitals

When you are in an intimate relationship, how do you communicate which types of touch you enjoy most?

_____Discuss it with my partner.

_____Assume he already knows.

_____Move his hands to show him.

_____Grunt and groan and wonder what to make for dinner.

_____Other_____

EXERCISES TO INCREASE YOUR TOUCH AWARENESS

Learning to value touch again.

1. Use a shower massage on different parts of your body. Try to really experience the different sensations as you alter the water's flow.
2. Fill a tub with warm water and bubbles and something that smells fabulous. Lie back. Concentrate on how the warm water alters the way your body feels over an extended period of time.

3. Gather some interesting objects: a pear, a hairbrush, something made out of silk, a down pillow, a stuffed animal. Close your eyes. Touch each object in turn, paying close attention to how each feels against your skin.

4. Play in your garden or with your plants. Pull out weeds or repot the plants or dig in the soil. How does the dirt feel in your hands?

5. Try flannel sheets. They are warm and soft to touch.

6. Touch your partner. Ask him to focus only on your touch. Then ask him to touch you so you can focus on his touch. Masters and Johnson referred to this as "sensate focus." It is not meant to be sexual—try touching body parts you typically do *not* touch. Find a time when you can relax and take your time. This kind of touching, in and of itself, can be a very erotic experience for many touch-starved Americans.

7. Touch the seasons. Jump in a leaf pile. Make a snow angel. Stroke the petals of a rose. Roll in the grass.

8. Play with children (or without them!) on the swings. Slide down the slide. Play with their play dough or clay.

9. Mix equal parts of cornstarch and water in a dishpan and have yourself an incredibly fun touching experience. Run your fingers through the "goop." Watch it change textures as it moves through your hands.

10. Sit in the sand at the beach and make sand castles. Sit on the driveway and write with sidewalk chalk. Feel the textures of a child's world. Children revel in touch and learn much about their world through this wonderful sense. We can, too!

SEEING

Try to see the same old things in new ways.

Touching is one of our senses that is often stifled and forgotten, while sight is one that we are bombarded with all day long. As a result, we become accustomed to so many things that we no longer see them. Although sight is not often considered as an important part of sex, it is usually the sense that stimulates an almost automatic response. The sight of your partner can stimulate you long before his touch does. To heighten your sense of sight, try these exercises:

1. Take a new route to work. Watch for all the new and different sights along the way.
2. Walk on the opposite side of the street for a few days. Look at people's gardens and landscaping. Smell their flowers while you're at it!
3. Rent an old movie you love but haven't seen in years. Better yet, rent an old musical and stimulate your hearing as well.
4. Go to your favorite clothing store and try on new outfits. Go for a look you've admired but have been afraid to try. Pay close attention to how your moods and attitudes change with the outfits.
5. Buy yourself a bouquet of flowers. Put them where you spend the most time—even if they end up on the kitchen counter.
6. Reward yourself with some candles. Group them together and light them one by one, watching how they change the atmosphere in the room.
7. Try some new and interesting garnishes on your dinner plates. Use fresh fruits and vegetables to bring color and texture to ordinary foods.
8. Spend some time in a women's locker room. Notice the great variety of women's bodies and the realities of aging. Notice how some women are open and comfortable with their nakedness while others try to hide themselves.
9. Recall a vision or setting that once gave you immense pleasure: a sunrise or sunset, a cloud formation, the sunlight through the trees, city lights reflected on a lake, the face of an elderly person or a baby. Try to describe this vision fully. Could you recreate it in your daily life?

Hearing

Try being kind and gentle to your hearing sense.

Hearing is our other sense that seems to be bombarded, but rarely do we take the time to nurture it. We hear the sounds of machines, automobiles, factories, telephones, boom boxes, and doorbells all day long. Do you remember the peace that can be found in certain sounds? The lack of any sounds?

Sound affects us sexually as well. When is the last time you made love with your favorite music playing? Or talked to your partner while you were having sex? For many women, what we hear before, during, and after sex can be an important part of the experience of sex itself. If you tune in carefully, you'll see how sound can increase your sensual awareness.

1. Buy a new CD or tape of relaxing, pleasant sounds like the ocean, a rainstorm, or the forest. Find a quiet place and listen for a few minutes. Notice how the sounds change your body and relax you.
2. Disconnect the phone for a few minutes every day, particularly when you want to concentrate on something or listen to music. They'll call back.
3. Take a hike through a forest or meadow. Take your children. I recently blindfolded my young sons, took their hands, and led them on a forest hike. They listened for all the sounds and noticed the smells. Since men tend to be so visual, this is a great way to nurture other senses in boys!
4. Go to the opera or another musical event. Try to hear the different instruments. Close your eyes and hear how each individual sound works with the others to form the whole.
5. Turn off the television!
6. Take the time to talk to your partner. Tell him what you like and don't like about what you both do during sex.
7. Identify two sounds you find offensive. Can you get away from them? How?

_____

_____

8. Name some sounds you find nurturing. Could you enjoy them more often?

_____

_____

_____

_____

SMELLING

How quickly smell can take us home!

The importance of the sense of smell struck home for me one day, a month or so after my husband had left the country on a six-month tour of duty, when I suddenly came across a shirt he had left hanging on a rack. As I picked it up to toss in the laundry, I was suddenly overcome by the smells. His cologne and body smells brought him back into the room so forcefully that I was momentarily overcome with my sense of loss. Certain other smells, like bread baking in the kitchen, pine wafting through the house as the Christmas tree is brought inside, or fresh powder on a baby's bottom, instantly transport us back to earlier places and times.

The sense of smell, so often forgotten in our day-to-day lives, is one of our most primeval instincts. It helped us survive in prehistoric times! One of the essential roles smell plays unto this day is to begin our hunger response. When we smell food, we begin to salivate and our stomach acids form. We have all had times when we weren't hungry at all, but the smell of popcorn at the movie theatre or chocolate chip cookies baking tempted us to eat anyway. This is a normal part of our biological makeup and is one reason smell is a difficult sense for many dieters, who become hypersensitive to the smells around them.

Nurturing our sense of smell through nonfood alternatives helps!

Smell some wonderful things that are NOT food.

1. Slowly peel an orange. Smell the fresh oils that are left on your hands.
2. Buy a new perfume and wear it only when you feel like nurturing yourself.
3. Fill your home with potpourris in your favorite scents.
4. Take a walk by the ocean or a lake or a stream on the day after a rainstorm. What smells different about the water and wind?
5. Identify one or two of your favorite smells. Why do you love them?

_____

_____

6. Do you surround yourself with pleasant smells or not even notice the smells around you?

TASTING

Tasting is an important sense in terms of our sensuality as well. Just as young children learn about their world by tasting everything they meet, we also learn about our partner through our sense of taste. How does a kiss on your partner's neck taste after he's been playing basketball as compared to being fresh out of the shower? My husband often teases me before he leaves for a long trip. As I bury my face in his neck he asks, "Honey, are you imprinting me again?" And yes, I believe there is some truth to that. It is as if I am operating on a primitive level to remember all I can about him!

Try tasting real food. Take a break from additives.

Taste is a problem sense for many Americans. We often wolf down our food so quickly on our way to somewhere else that we don't consciously stop to taste it. In addition, many of us have lost our ability to distinguish real tastes from chemical additives. When was the last time you tasted something truly profound—a taste that made your taste buds stand up and take notice?

Here are a few ways to heighten your taste experiences:

1. Experiment with new flavors to awaken your taste buds.

• Add a bit of gorgonzola cheese to your pizza.
• Add garlic cloves to the water while you boil potatoes.
• Chop fresh chives into your pasta.
• Pour some red pepper sauce on your cooked legumes.
• Try fresh basil mixed with your salad greens.
• Add fresh cilantro to your tacos or burritos.
• Try dijon mustard in your chicken breast marinade.
• Add horseradish to your dips and sauces.
• Roll lean steaks in freshly ground pepper.
• Try a bit of extra virgin olive oil mixed with some of the new vinegars in your salad dressings.

There are many, many ways to increase flavors in foods without adding additional fat or calories. These foods will taste so alive that you will feel fulfilled with much smaller amounts!

Decrease the fat and taste the flavors . . .

2. Cut out extra fats and sauces in your recipes and replace them with vibrant flavors. Once you get used to the flavor of fat, it is hard to notice other flavors. Our American hamburger is a good example. Next time, buy the leanest ground beef you can afford and combine it with ¼ cup each of grated carrots, minced green pepper, and diced onions. Grill it for a wonderfully flavored, juicy, lower fat, higher nutrient burger.
3. Choose fresh foods whenever possible. Eat what is in season. Canned and frozen foods just aren't as satisfying.

We are multidimensional human beings employing intricate biological mechanisms to survive. Our senses played a vital role in ensuring our survival long before the onset of one-dimensional media such as television, books, and computer screens. Neglecting and ignoring the senses is a certain step away from the enjoyment of our physical bodies as they were meant to be. Relying on our visual sense to process all of our information can result in negative thinking about our bodies and the many things they were created for.

Enjoy your senses and your sensuality.

Nurturing your senses—*all* of your senses—is one of the most important things you can do for yourself. In addition to fine-tuning your mind-body connection, nurturing your senses helps you understand what gives you physical pleasure. Enjoy your senses and your sensuality—together, they will lead you to your feminine spirit and free you to enjoy your own sexuality for the rest of your life.

What You Can Do Right Now

1. Focus on one sense today. Nurture it, pamper it, and discover what is offensive and what is enjoyable to that sense.
2. Share with your partner what you like and don't like about sex. Discuss with him your view of your own sexuality that you developed in this step.

Define the Many Roles in Your Life

Spiritual and religious traditions, when shaped by the feminine principle, affirm the cyclical phases of our lives and the wisdom each phase brings, the sacredness of our bodies and the body of the Earth.

—PATRICIA WYNNE

In the previous chapters, we've taken some difficult and sometimes painstaking looks at the external forces that have been destructive in our relationships with our bodies. We have seen how the media, advertising, the diet mongers, our culture, and even significant others in our lives have influenced the way we see ourselves and our behaviors. With this next step, it's time to leave all that baggage behind and move on toward creating our own road maps for the future and learning more about who we truly are as individuals.

Dieting, thinness, exercise, the perfect man, a great job, silicone breasts—none of these can make us truly happy for the long term. Real happiness stems from a passion for life, an appreciation of the world, and peace with who we are as individuals. Because it comes from within, that is where we must focus our resources.

The first step in the process of looking toward a future of loving your body and yourself is to determine who you are independent of the other people in your life. As women, we fulfill many roles as nurturers, mothers, daughters, sisters, lovers, wives, employees, employers, chairpersons, friends, and others. In the busyness of our lives, we don't often take the opportunity to see how these roles all fit into our goals, whether these roles still fit well for us, and what they teach us about our inner selves.

In this chapter you will begin to figure out who *you* are. The exercises on the following pages will help you evaluate your strengths and weaknesses. Because they are lengthy and thought-provoking, you may wish to do them once and set them aside, coming back later to review what you wrote before moving on. The information you gain here will enable you to weigh your resources against your concerns and, if necessary, start defining your roles so that you can continue moving forward.

Who Am I?

1. Uniqueness: Who am I?
Write a few sentences that sum up your sense of who you are and what makes you unique in this world. What distinguishes you from others? Do others see you the same way you see yourself? Do you have a clear picture of who you are as an individual, or are there times when you lose your sense of uniqueness and feel confused about your identity?

_____

_____

_____

_____

_____

continued

2. Ability: What do I do well?

Do you see yourself as someone who can achieve goals? Do you have the resources you need to accomplish them? Use the column on the left to list areas where you feel you do well. Use the column on the right to list areas of your life where you feel you could do better.

_____   _____

_____   _____

_____   _____

_____   _____

_____   _____

3. Self-sufficiency: How do I do on my own?

Are you able to work independently and get things done on your own? What situations cause you to ask for help? In the column on the left, list the situations in your life where you tend to be independent. In the column on the right, list areas where you tend to need help from others.

_____   _____

_____   _____

_____   _____

_____   _____

_____   _____

continued

4. Principles: What do I believe in?
List the guiding principles or values that you use to navigate the direction your life takes. What is important to you? How do you live your values in your daily life?

_____

_____

_____

_____

5. Companionship: What are my close relationships like?
How comfortable do you feel getting close to other people? Do you have a good mix of acquaintances, friends, and intimate relationships? Try to sum up your relationships in a few sentences. Include how you feel about your peers and other social groups in your life. Also evaluate whether you are outgoing or reserved in social situations.

_____

_____

_____

_____

_____

continued

6. Sexuality: What is my sexual nature?

How satisfied are you with your sexuality and your sexual choices? What about your sexual relationships? Are you comfortable with your sexuality in both public and private settings? See if you can capture the essence of your sexual nature in two or three sentences.

_____

_____

_____

_____

7. Commitments: How do I feel about those closest to me?

Are you in a satisfying marriage or long-term relationship? If not, are you content with not being part of a couple? How do you get along with your family and siblings? How do you feel about your children? If you are not a parent, do you look forward to becoming one, or do you have misgivings?

_____

_____

_____

_____

continued

8. Career: How do I feel about my life's work?
Does your work bring you joy, or are there things about your job you would like to change? Do you make a difference because of your work? How does your workplace feel? Do you need to change careers?

_____

_____

_____

_____

9. Community: What am I returning?
Write a few sentences about how you use your time and re-sources in the community outside of your friends, work, and family. Are you involved in your neighborhood, school, church, or political groups? Do you feel upbeat about the world today or pessimistic? Do you believe you can make a difference?

_____

_____

_____

_____

continued

10. Leisure: How do I spend my free time?
Do you take time to relax and enjoy life? Do you pursue your
own creative interests? What do you get out of your leisure time?
Could you benefit from giving yourself more time to slow down
and relax?

_____

_____

_____

_____

_____

_____

11. Learning: How do I challenge myself?
Evaluate your attitudes toward continuing to learn for the rest of
your life. Are you challenging yourself by reading, taking
courses, or learning new skills? Are you stuck? What new skills
could help you?

_____

_____

_____

_____

_____

_____

continued

12. Summarize who you are.
Look back at what you wrote. Pick out the strengths that will help you most in life and look for problem areas that may stand in the way of your becoming a full person. Try to summarize who you are.

_____

_____

_____

The Wheel of Your Life

Get a visual sense of the many roles in your life.

If you are like most women, you play multiple roles in your life. Sometimes, the roles conflict. When this happens, it can be very difficult to determine which will take priority. Looking at this visually can help you define what roles you play, how they conflict, and who you are in relation to others. You should also get a clearer sense of which roles make you happiest.

Begin this exercise by *writing your name in the center of the wheel opposite. At the end of each spoke, write your role* as it relates to others: mother, wife, daughter, sister, friend, student, job title, and so forth. Think clearly through *all* areas of your life so you do not omit any of your roles. If you need to, you can add more spokes to your wheel. After you have named your roles, fill in the space below each one with a *description of some of the demands and expectations* that role places on you. Here are a few examples:

Daughter
My mother calls three times a week and expects me to be available to chat.
I am expected to be at all family functions.

Professional
My boss expects me to learn how to use the new computer.
Some of the people at work think I am antisocial because I don't drink beer with them after work on Fridays.
I am behind on several projects.

Looking back at your roles, put a #1 next to the role that is your source of greatest happiness and brings you the most pleasure. Next, find the role that most clearly allows you to be yourself, and put a star next to it. This should be the role that you feel comfortable about yourself in—the one that energizes you. Were the two roles the same? Were they different? Why or why not?

Roles can help us define ourselves by putting us in the context of the larger world beyond ourselves. Attempt to sit through a conversation for an hour with a group of mothers of young children when you have none and you'll quickly see how a role can provide definition! Or on the same note, spend an hour as a single person with a group of couples and it becomes easy to understand how relationships with others define us.

The downside is, this external definition of ourselves can cause problems. Spending too much time in one role can be limiting to our view of the wider world. Our roles can also limit us in our growth as individuals. What mother of young children did not want to escape for a day (or perhaps much longer!) to a warm, tranquil beach? How many times do you go home to visit and find the only thing that has changed is the color of the wallpaper? Many women also find conflict among their various roles. Yes, perhaps you'd love to escape to the beach for a while, but what would become of the children? And if you chose not to go home because your parents' perception of you never changes, what would be the repercussions?

Each role places separate and unique demands on you. When these roles conflict, they can often cause you to feel guilty and overwhelmed because you cannot fulfill everyone's expectations. This, in turn, can keep you from hearing your body's messages and nurturing your own body's needs.

Look carefully at your wheel. Try to identify the conflicts that exist among your roles. Here are a few examples:

I am missing deadlines at work, but my children need me to drive them to baseball practice.
I can't socialize with my friends because I am too tired after working all day.
My husband thinks I spend too much time at work for too little pay.

In the space below, identify your own conflicts among your roles:

_____
_____
_____
_____

_____

_____

_____

You can lessen the impact of role conflicts.

After you have identified the conflicts among your roles, think about what could be done to cause fewer conflicts between what you want in your life and what others want from you. For example, is it time to discuss your workload with your boss? Could your husband or children help more with household chores? Could you let some of your roles, like PTA president or committee member, go?

Some steps you could take are:

_____

_____

_____

_____

_____

_____

_____

Read through your list of conflicts. Which *two* are most urgent? Would you be willing to change? Try to pick the two that would afford you more control in other areas and bring you more enjoyment.

1. _____

2. _____

How do you see your body—as a vehicle or as a friend?

By clearly defining our roles, we can see how little time we have left to care for our bodies in the way they need. Many of us are so busy nurturing others that we often have little if any time left to nurture ourselves. Our bodies are reduced to vehicles that help us accomplish the day's tasks. We do not treat them as the vital, joyful friends that they are.

Are you a "toxic waste dump"?

In learning about ourselves and our relationships to others in our life, we need to take a hard look at how other people can affect the way we feel about ourselves. This is a difficult but essential task on the road to learning to love our bodies. Women tend to be such nurturers and providers for others that we don't stop long enough to put our needs first. By learning to recognize where our energy goes and where we gain it from, we can begin to establish boundaries between ourselves and others.

The people in our lives can be divided into two groups: the toxic people and the supportive ones. A toxic person is one who drains us of our energy stores. Toxic people take more from us than they give; they leave us feeling spent and emotionally drained after we have been with them. I often refer to them as the "bloodsuckers" of our lives.

Toxic people can take many different places in our lives. I have had several "friends" through the years who eventually became toxic to my self-growth. One "friend" in particular stays clearly in my mind. We had a standing appointment once a week for coffee. Each time we met over the course of a year's time, the discussion routinely revolved around whether or not she should divorce her husband.

"Oh, I just don't know what to do. We haven't gotten along in years, and he doesn't support my work at all, but I worry so about the kids. And what would happen to him if I left him?" After several months of monopolized conversation regarding this dilemma, I realized that I left each week feeling drained, upset, and as if my friendship was being abused. Rarely if ever did the topic of what was going on in my life come up, and if it did, it was only to get my opinion. It was evident she needed to make a decision one way or another, but to use the time we were together to lament this situation left me feeling used and unimportant. When I realized this friend had become toxic to me, I ceased our morning coffees and my embroilment in her indecisiveness.

We all have people in our lives who take our best and leave the rest. One of my workshop participants laughed at the thought she could ever have a toxic person in her life. "Ha," she said, "there is no one I would allow to take my spirit away from me." The next week she humbly handed me a slip of paper with five names on it. "I guess you're right. I do have some toxic people in my life, although it took me really sitting down to think about it."

Toxic people can be covert. They may be as near to us as our siblings, parents, coworkers, or even friends. Toxic people can also be as distant from us as the media pressuring us to conform to a specific body size or the teller at the bank who always greets us with a frown and a negative attitude.

Supportive people in our lives are our lifeblood. These are the people who affirm for us the richness and esteem of our lives and are there for us in every way possible. When clients are struggling to decide who might fit on this often very short list, I ask them to recall who it is in their lives they could wake up at three in the morning with a phone call to talk. Or another way to look at it: for whom would you jump in front of a moving truck to save their life? Ah, now you see why this list is often so very short. Few people in our lives can or will fulfill this role. Supportive people are not judgmental; they care for our happiness and our concerns and support us through the steps in our journey.

Now give some thought to those in your life who are the toxic people and those who are your supporters.

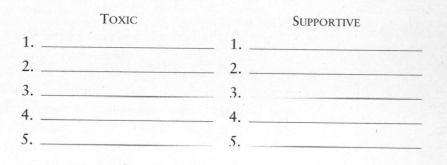

TOXIC

1. _____
2. _____
3. _____
4. _____
5. _____

SUPPORTIVE

1. _____
2. _____
3. _____
4. _____
5. _____

How do the toxic people on your list drain your energy?

_____

_____

_____

How do your supportive people enable you to be more effective?

_____

_____

_____

Which list is longer, and what does that say about you?

_____

_____

_____

By now, I am sure it is becoming clear that the majority of your time should be spent with your supportive people, and you should be with your toxic people as little as possible. Are there toxic people you can decide *not* to involve in your life so much?

As in the example of my "friend," it is important to set boundaries on our relationships with toxic people. Because she was supposedly my friend, it was not apparent to me for some time that I was wasting essential life energy on this relationship. The sooner you can set a boundary between yourself and a toxic person, the healthier.

Establishing a boundary between yourself and those who drain you can be a very difficult situation for a woman who has been raised not to show her true feelings. By creating our own boundaries, we can garner some control over otherwise hurtful situations.

Suppose you had a friend who called you repeatedly during your family's dinner hour to complain about her job. As time wears on, this type of person can leave you feeling angry and resentful over lost family time. You decide that a boundary must be established, and the next time she calls you tell her, "Jane, your calls during dinner are taking away from the time I spend with my family. I need to ask that you call me at . . . [another time more appropriate for you]."

When I was younger, I had a boss so toxic to me that in the hour prior to our weekly meetings I found myself plagued with severe diarrhea and stomach cramping. I could not believe the toxicity this woman created in my life. The main problem was that almost everything she said was a lie or a great exaggeration of the truth, and as I had been raised to be honest and truthful, this person's behavior conflicted with my inner value system.

Over time, I learned to tape every meeting I had with her. I kept copious notes of our meetings and had her initial everything that was presented to her. I chose to keep myself out of the rumor mill and rarely spoke about anything that was personal, so as not to provide grist for the mill. The stress of working in a system that was in such opposition to my values eventually led to my resignation, as I determined I could not grow or ever prosper in that environment. Establishing boundaries can preserve our energy, creativity, and self-esteem in the midst of toxic people.

You may find, as many do, that there are people in your life who fit under both headings. Clients often list their mothers under both headings, perhaps because of the sometimes confusing and complicated relationships we have with them. Husbands or boyfriends may be seen under both. The men in our closest relationships can at once be supportive and loving, and the next hour be a source of our greatest frustration and anger. The key is to look for those who fit exclusively under one column or the other, and be mindful of how you manage your time with these people.

You may wish to review this column during the coming days and add names. During your daily activities it will become apparent who fits under which heading. Also, remember that your supportive people will provide you with invaluable resources as you move from here into creating your vision of the future.

Defining the Real You

As these exercises have shown, the relationships in our external world can affect the way we think about and see ourselves. They can also undermine our life goals and energy, draining us of the resources we need to love our own bodies and care for them first.

In this next step, we will move from the outside world of your life into the inner you. These exercises are designed to expand on what you already know about yourself, working for a clearer definition of your uniqueness as an individual. The first set of exercises will assess your problem areas, and the second step will expand on your strengths.

*Where do you
need to make
changes?*

Problem Areas in My Life

Do the following sentence-completion exercises as quickly as
you can. Write down the very first response that pops into your
mind. Do not stop to think about your responses or try to judge
them beforehand.

1. My biggest problem in life is _____

   _____

   _____

2. Another one of my concerns is _____

   _____

   _____

3. Something I do that causes me problems is _____

   _____

   _____

4. Something I don't do that causes me problems is _____

   _____

   _____

5. I feel most negative about my life when _____

   _____

   _____

6. The person I have the most conflict with is _____

   _____

   _____

continued

7. The thing that troubles me most about this relationship is

_____

_____

8. My life would be much better if_____

_____

_____

9. I have a difficult time coping with_____

_____

_____

10. I become the most anxious when_____

_____

_____

11. A value that I don't put into practice is_____

_____

_____

12. I'm most afraid of_____

_____

_____

13. I wish I_____

_____

_____

continued

14. I wish I did not _____

_____

_____

15. The thing about me that others dislike most is_____

_____

_____

16. The one thing I don't seem to handle very well is_____

_____

_____

17. I don't seem to have the skills to_____

_____

_____

18. A problem I keep having, over and over, is_____

_____

_____

19. If I could change one thing about myself it would be_____

_____

_____

Your five weakest areas.

Take a few minutes to look over your answers. After thinking about what you wrote, name the five things that you feel are your weakest areas:

1. _____

2. _____

3. _____

4. _____

5. _____

*Learning more
about your
strengths.*

Strengths in My Life

Now look at your strong points. Again, you need to do the
following sentence-completion exercises as quickly as you can.
Write down the very first response that pops into your mind.

1. The thing I like best about myself is _____
_____
_____

2. The thing others like best about me is _____
_____
_____

3. The thing I do best in life is _____
_____
_____

4. A recent problem I've handled well is _____
_____
_____

5. I'm at my best when _____
_____
_____

6. I'm glad that I _____
_____
_____

continued

7. A compliment that was recently paid to me is _____
_____
_____

8. A value that I practice is _____
_____
_____

9. An example of how I care about others is _____
_____
_____

10. Others can depend on me to _____
_____
_____

11. Something I'm handling better this year than last is ___
_____
_____

12. One obstacle in my life that I've overcome is _____
_____
_____

13. An example of my ability to handle life is _____
_____
_____

continued

14. An example of how dependable I am is_____
_____
_____

15. I have the guts to_____
_____
_____

16. I'm best with people when I'm_____
_____
_____

17. One good thing I've done for my body in the last year is
_____
_____

18. My greatest accomplishment at this point in my life is_____
_____
_____

19. One important goal I intend to act on within two months is
_____
_____

Your five strongest areas:

Take a few minutes to look over your answers. After thinking about what you wrote, name the five things that you think are your most positive strengths:

1._____
2._____
3._____
4._____
5._____

How could you use these strengths to manage other problem areas in your life, especially your role conflicts?

Are you beginning to see the real you?

In the coming days, you should continue to think about ways you might be able to define your roles. Try to find your comfort zone, that place where you are challenged but not overstressed. Make taking care of your body and your individual needs a top priority in your life. Eat plenty of good food to keep your energy levels high and to serve as a reminder that you are taking charge of your own life.

By working through the exercises in this chapter, you have started to rediscover your inner self—not the you that has been trying to be thinner or less fat or more beautiful in someone else's eyes, but the real you. By defining your roles and assessing your strengths and weaknesses, you can learn to draw your own map of where you want to go in life. The map that kept you chasing after thinness and unrealistic social models led to nothing but dead ends and detours. The map you make for yourself will show you exactly how to get where you want to be.

What You Can Do Right Now

1. Discuss your role conflicts with a close friend or family member. Be especially open to suggestions/feedback on how to enlist the support of others. What would you lose by delegating some of your workload?

2. Continue to refine your roles. Are you doing what *you* want to do or what others want you to do? Remind yourself that it is impossible to be "everything to everyone."

3. Keep a close eye out for all the toxic people in your life. Say "thank you" to one of your supportive people for being there for you!

Develop a Philosophy of Balance

We need time to dream, time to remember, and time to reach the infinite. Time to be.

—GLADYS TABER

It isn't until you come to a spiritual understanding of who you are—not necessarily a religious feeling, but deep down, the spirit within—that you can begin to take control.

—OPRAH WINFREY

Are you a "go-for-broke" gambler?

Think of your time and energy as money, and try to calculate how much a month you've been spending on counting calories and fat grams, reading diet books, overexercising, and beating yourself up over your failure to be thinner than you are. Now add in the time you've spent *thinking* about what to eat or not to eat, when and how much to exercise, and everything else related to the pursuit of a thinner body. You are probably talking about a substantial chunk of change.

Take all those coins and drop them into a slot machine where the odds of winning the jackpot are only two in a hundred. Worse yet, the two "winners" have been genetically selected beforehand. Unless you are the thin, bony type to start with, you're an automatic loser.

126

What are the odds of hitting the thin jackpot?

That is pretty much how the "get thin" game is played. We are lured into squandering our internal resources on the long-shot chance we'll hit the thin jackpot.

Once you start loving the body you were born with, you will be free of the compulsion to waste your resources. You'll be able to spend your time and energy on things with much more tangible, permanent rewards. The exercises that follow will help you budget and invest your "new" personal resources so you end up with a healthy balance in all three of your personal accounts: mind, body, and spirit.

Are all parts of you in harmony?

All parts of your being must be in harmony for you to function as a complete human being. Many women I have worked with over the years have all but forgotten some of their components in the pursuit of a thinner body. One woman told me she had come from a deeply religious family, but she had been "so busy working out at the gym" for so many years that she had forgotten about her spiritual side until I mentioned it.

Likewise, spending every waking hour wrapped up in work or school can detract from the personal side of life. Not paying attention to all parts of our whole can lead us to be irritable or frustrated or feel that we lack a sense of purpose. We all need balance in our lives. To attain that balance, we need to nurture our bodies, our minds, and our spirits.

Look at the many ways to nurture your body.

How Balanced Is My Life?

In order to assess how balanced your life is, look at each area and think about how you have nurtured or ignored development in that part of your being. This exercise will help you begin to think about what parts of you are being attended to and what parts are not. Put a check mark next to any activity you have done in the last month.

continued

Physical (Body)

_____Had a massage?

_____Caught a fish?

_____Spent thirty minutes exercising in your target heart zone?

_____Chose a salad instead of a burger?

_____Had your blood pressure or cholesterol checked?

_____Bought a new outfit?

_____Had a leaf fight or snowball fight?

_____Ate five fruits or vegetables in one day?

_____Took a bubble bath?

_____Rocked in a rocking chair?

_____Ate a sucker?

_____Made an overdue appointment for a physical or the dentist?

_____Flossed your teeth?

_____Didn't set the alarm clock?

_____Learned a new sport?

Emotional (Mind)

_____Cried?

_____Laughed 'til your belly ached?

_____Made a new friend?

_____Journaled?

_____Said no?

_____Asked for what you wanted?

_____Positively expressed your anger?

_____Spent one uninterrupted hour with your partner or child?

_____Did one positive thing for the environment?

_____Had a political discussion?

_____Volunteered somewhere for an hour?

continued

Who is minding YOUR needs?

_____ Hugged someone outside your family?
_____ Took a class to learn something new?
_____ Read a new book?
_____ Watched a documentary on television?
_____ Visited somewhere you'd never been?
_____ Wrote a letter by hand to a friend?
_____ Gave a compliment to a stranger?
_____ Apologized for something and really meant it?

Spiritual (Spirit)

_____ Spoke with your Higher Power?
_____ Practiced yoga?
_____ Hiked through the woods?
_____ Meditated?
_____ Smelled a campfire?
_____ Lay on a blanket and looked at the stars?
_____ Discussed a dream with someone?
_____ Lay in the grass and watched the clouds?
_____ Lit a candle and waited for the wax to melt?
_____ Listened to instrumental-only music?

Nurturing our spiritual side gives meaning to our everyday existence.

Which parts of you need nurturing?

How many check marks did you have in each area? Could you see at a glance if you were neglecting one area of your total self? These questions were admittedly quirky—not at all scientific—but they hopefully stimulated your imagination and gave you ideas on how to nurture each area.

This next exercise is more quantifiable. Begin by looking at the circle on page 131. You can see it has three broad categories:

The physical component includes all areas of your life that relate to the care and well-being of your body, including such things as your eating and hygiene habits, how much you exercise, your stress management skills, and your medical history and status.

The spiritual component covers your philosophy of life, your dreams, and all matters connected with spiritual ritual and reflection.

The emotional component includes all of your intellectual and feelings-related areas, including your interpersonal skills. How you express your feelings and creativity, your relationships with your spouse and children, and the major aspects of your professional life are all included here.

To complete this exercise, you need to work through each of the components by evaluating how much time and energy you give to nurturing each aspect of your life.

Using a scale of 1 to 10, assign a number to each subcategory in the circle. For example, if you are starting in the Physical section, find the Sleep Habits subcategory.

Use a scale of 1 to 10 to evaluate each area of your life.

- 1 indicates you never get enough sleep.
- 5 means you try to get a decent night's rest most of the time.
- 10 indicates you sleep too much. (I know, not common!)

Do this for each subcategory in each of the three sections. Once you have finished the subcategories, locate the arrows that come from the center and point to each larger category. Shade in as much of that section of the arrow as you feel suits the amount of attention you pay yourself in that area. The 50 percent and 100 percent markers are drawn for you—within those levels, try to shade as close to your figures as you can. Review all the numbers in your subcategories to draw a general conclusion about each of the three larger categories.

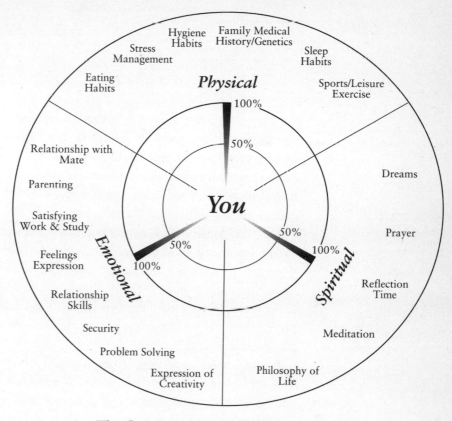

The Components of a Well-rounded You

When you see your completed circle, how well balanced does your life look?

_____

_____

_____

What areas do you spend a lot of time caring for?

_____

_____

_____

What areas do you tend to neglect?

_____

_____

_____

Every day more research comes to us about the mind/body/spirit connection. This research clearly shows that there is much we don't know yet about the potential power of human beings. Ignoring one area creates an unbalance in the entire system. In an age when technology is increasing at such incredible rates, it is more important than ever to seek balance in all aspects of our lives.

Go back to the check marks you made on the previous pages under "How Balanced Is My Life?" and review them. Are there things in those lists you didn't check but would nonetheless love to do? Highlight them. Incorporate them into your daily living. Each step you make toward a more balanced life will help you in learning to love your body and in investing your valuable resources in jackpots that pay true rewards.

Entire books have been written about most of the titles under the subcategories. There are many books available on such topics as parenting, stress management, self-defense, and renewing your soul. Although each book or program can help in working through problems in a specific area, they don't help in looking at the bigger, overall picture.

Expression of Creativity

In my work with women over the years, I routinely see two of the subcategories virtually ignored: one is the expression of creativity, and the other is developing a philosophy of life.

Initially, I would hear this recurring question somewhere in the back of my mind when working with a client: "How does she have time to count every calorie?" or "How can she possibly have a balanced life spending one hour in the gym and running ten miles every day?" Over time it became obvious to me that the majority of the women I saw (particularly the young women) had been robbed of their creativity somewhere along the line. They had been so busy going to school, building careers and/or families that they hadn't taken the time to nurture their own life-giving creative forces.

I once made this statement in a keynote address I was giving for a state meeting of home economics educators. I was overwhelmed with the standing ovation they gave me! The audience broke into chaos with questions and comments about the young women they worked with on a daily basis. These educators felt that this was the essence of many of the problems they were seeing with their students. Dieting, weight loss, starvation, and exercise had robbed these young women of the self-esteem and sense of productivity that creative ventures provide for them.

Imagine growing up in ancient China and having your toes bound to the soles of your feet from the age of four or five. Eventually, the scabbing and lesions wear away and the young growing foot becomes deformed to the point that the young woman is unable to walk, dependent on others to do her work for her and control her life. This example, although dramatic, is not much different from the world young women grow up in here, today. Bound from an early age in the belief that "thinness equals success and happiness," the young woman's every moment is spent concerned with her looks, her body, and her size. Her self-esteem and belief in her own power eventually form scabs after repeatedly receiving messages that she is not thin enough or not good enough. Under a regimen of inadequate food and liquids, she surrenders control of her life to others who will care for her and ensure her future. Is it no wonder that these young girls have difficulty expressing creativity in their lives?

Unwrapping the bandages and bindings takes time. The muscles are weak and need special exercises. The mind may feel uncomfortable faced with this seemingly insurmountable task, akin to the feeling the young Chinese girl must feel when trying to walk after her feet have been bound for years.

As women, creativity is a vital part of our lives, but it demands constant attention. Our creative ability can be our most valuable asset, because it gives outwardly and feeds inwardly at every level: spiritually, mentally, emotionally, and economically. Ideally, our creative energies should have no walls or boundaries.

Has your creative flow been "dammed"?

Creative juices flow from within us; they rise, roll, and incubate. The only way to avoid the insistent energy is to mount barriers against it or allow it to be poisoned. When a woman does not like the image she sees in the mirror, she can be attacked and crippled at her core. The message she hears is "You are not good enough. What comes from within you is not adequate." She begins to lose trust in the creative forces that drive her life. Chasing after an unattainable ideal of thinness is one of the cruelest ways to rape a woman's creative energies and rob her of her life-giving forces.

Creativity is an essential part of human nature—another type of evolutionary mechanism that has helped humans to survive. Our environment is in constant flux, and our creativity is essential in helping us to respond to or influence these changes. Creativity allows us to constantly remake ourselves and remodel our behaviors to best fit new conditions or sometimes shape these new conditions. This is why creativity is the core of changing the way you feel about yourself and your body.

Your inner creativity can help you respond successfully to change. Creativity can be a wellspring of new ideas that you can use to:

- be more efficient and productive
- feel more powerful and self-confident in your life
- make your life more interesting and exciting

Creativity is a process of responding to old, tired situations in new ways. You can use your creativity to do anything in your life, including reshaping your views about yourself and your relationships with others, refashioning your work environment, or society as a whole; you may also choose to create different forms of artistic expression. In order to nurture your creative forces, you must understand the keys to creativity.

1. Creativity is the ability to feel and think in innovative ways. It is an approach that helps you develop new ideas by using techniques such as brainstorming and paying attention to your gut responses or intuition to find alternatives or new solutions.

2. Creativity is an openness to looking at different ways of doing things; it allows you to be willing to accept new ideas and to act on them.
3. Creativity can give you the insight to see which areas of your life can be affected by being creative and which areas don't need to be changed.

Creativity can be many things to many different women. One woman may find that playing a musical instrument nurtures her creativity, while another may find that writing computer software nurtures hers. Some women enjoy more challenging creative pursuits, while others may prefer more mundane activities. The point is that you must find those things that allow your creativity to flow, and nurture them.

What does creativity mean to you?

_____

_____

_____

What do you find nurtures your creativity?

_____

_____

_____

What robs you of your creativity?

_____

_____

_____

What kinds of energy do you receive from your creative ventures?

_____

_____

_____

List two or three creative pursuits that you love:

1. _____
2. _____
3. _____

Is there anything on your list that you want to learn, but you haven't yet?

Now, pick one from your list and get those creative juices flowing today!

Is your creativity calling you to come out and play?

Creativity can ebb and flow during different life stages, but it is always there waiting to resurge. There are a thousand different outlets for creative energy, and once you love the body you were born with, you will hear them calling you to come out and play. It makes no difference whether you choose an individual pursuit like painting, calligraphy, or journal writing, or a larger social pursuit like working for recycling in your neighborhood or changing the male face of American politics by running for office. Trust *your* creative forces!

Philosophy of Life

The second area that I see so many clients inattentive to is their philosophy of life. In accepting cultural, familial, or social expectations that have been defined for us, our basic philosophy of life becomes forgotten. For many, there may never have been an opportunity to actually take the time to write about and identify what is important in life. It is impossible to approach life from a balanced perspective if we don't understand what drives our lives to begin with.

Many things define who you are . . .

Who are you? If someone asked you, how would you define yourself?

By your roles?
I'm Paul's mom.
I'm Rod's wife.
I'm a reference librarian.
I'm the treasurer of my parish council.

By your beliefs?
   I'm a Christian.
   I follow the teachings of Mohammed.
   I'm a Republican.
   I support national health care.

By your interests?
   I'm an avid reader.
   I play golf.
   I've got a green thumb.
   I love to dance.

By your personality?
   I'm an introvert.
   I'm a take-charge kind of person.
   I'm the life of the party.
   I'm a good listener.

By your character?
   I'm always honest.
   I'm loyal to my family.
   I'm a hard worker.
   I try to help other people.

Do you add up your strengths and subtract your weaknesses? Are you the sum of your experiences? your possessions? the choices you've made? What about your thoughts, hopes, dreams, and fears?

If someone asked you who you were, your answer would probably depend upon who you were talking to, the context of the question, and how you felt at the moment. Your response might be similar to one of the common, off-the-cuff responses above, or it might be something entirely different. One thing, however, is certain. You would never dream of *defining* yourself—or anyone else, for that matter—by body size:

. . . and your body size is not one of them!

   I weigh 125 pounds.
   I wear a size 14.
   I'm not thin enough.

In the big picture of life, body size is insignificant. What do numbers on a scale have to do with who you are, what you believe, where you are going? What does your dress size have to do with your long-term happiness?

To love the body you were born with, you must keep your life in perspective. One of the best ways to do this is to pull together all of the important points you have covered thus far and use them to develop your own balanced philosophy of life. Your philosophy of life can help you to understand why you may have been neglecting areas of life we saw in the balance exercise earlier. It can also help create for you a foundation that includes balancing all areas of your life. It's not a simple task, but a little work now can give you a solid, tangible foundation on which to build the rest of your life.

As you set about this task, keep in mind that your philosophy will not be set in stone. Your particular beliefs will undoubtedly change over time, just as you will. Unforeseen events will alter your perspective, and even your basic path may veer. Still, it is important to develop your philosophy as clearly and concisely as you can.

"Universals" apply to all humans.

The sentences on the following pages will give you a framework. The boldface statements refer to "universals"—concepts that apply to all humans. Immediately below these are statements that apply specifically to you. Some of you will be able to zip through this in one sitting; your answers will come easily. Others may find it a struggle. If you need to, set it aside and come back to it in a day or a week. You may even want to discuss it with someone close to you. Just be prepared to reread, rewrite, and rethink as you go. Do not be in a hurry—there is no right way or wrong way to develop your philosophy. Only your way.

What Do I Believe?

You may want to review your value statements in the last chapter before beginning this exercise.

What are your most basic beliefs?

1. We have the free choice to choose what we want to be.

As a person, I want to be_____

_____

_____

2. Purpose and meaning are self-created; they are essential to inner peace and fulfillment.

My purpose in life is_____

_____

_____

3. We each develop our own beliefs.

I believe that_____

_____

_____

4. Change is a fact of life, whether it be living, growing, or dying.

The direction for my life today and tomorrow is_____

_____

_____

continued

5. Love is the most powerful force in life.

My ability to love is _____

_____

_____

6. Questions, challenges, and problems in life are essential to a positive self-image and to happiness.

I question _____

_____

_____

I have been challenged by _____

_____

_____

I have had problems when _____

_____

_____

7. Humans have potential for being either good or evil.

I am basically _____

_____

_____

8. All things in life are interconnected.

My ability to live in harmony with other things is _____

_____

_____

continued

9. All things in life can have a positive side.

I have been able to grow from problems in my life by_____

_____

_____

10. All people are the same, yet each individual is unique and special.

I am unique because_____

_____

_____

What brings meaning to your life?

11. If it can be imagined, it can be lived.

What I imagine can lead me to_____

_____

_____

12. Self-identity comes from observing, comparing, deciding, and responding to experience.

My self-identity will develop as I_____

_____

_____

13. Being at peace with oneself brings out the best in one's self.

My stability comes from_____

_____

_____

continued

14. We create our own feelings and emotional responses.

My feelings and responses come by _____

_____

_____

15. We all have basic drives in life.

The things that drive me are _____

_____

_____

My priorities are _____

_____

_____

Let your thoughts incubate.

When you have finished completing the sentences about your personal beliefs, set them aside for a while. Keep them in the back of your mind as you read, spend time with yourself, watch movies, and talk to others. Next time you read over your beliefs, you may want to add to what you have already written. When you feel you have nothing more to say, it will be time to write out a summary of your philosophy of life.

MY PHILOSOPHY OF LIFE

_____

_____

_____

_____

_____

_____

_____

_____

_____

_____

_____

_____

_____

_____

_____

_____

_____

_____

_____

_____

Your philosophy can help you set the goals you want.

Read over your philosophy summary several times. You need to know what it says without looking at it. You may even want to keep it with your personal journal (if you keep one) so you can review it at the beginning of each new year. It can be a wonderful tool for helping you set both long and short-term goals. It is also a clear reminder of who you really are.

Reflect back on the philosophy statement you've written. How can it help you maintain balance in the emotional, physical, and spiritual aspects of your life?

_____

_____

What essential values in your life have you neglected in light of other priorities?

_____

_____

These exercises may have been difficult and thought-provoking. For many of you, it may have been the first time you've had the opportunity to identify these critical aspects about yourself on paper. But these steps were important in providing a foundation for understanding your inner self better. You've had the chance to look inside yourself to learn more about what makes you tick and what is unique about you as an individual rather than a dress size. Using these universals as the foundation for your life will help you focus on the journey ahead instead of on your diet plans for today.

Equipped with your philosophy statement, a clear view of the roles in your life, knowledge of where your life is balanced and unbalanced, and an assessment of your strengths and weaknesses, it is now time to use your creative energies to move toward the future. In the final step of learning to love your body again, you will design a road map of your future by developing goals and an action plan for your life.

What You Can Do Right Now

Copy your philosophy statement and put it where you will see it often. Reread it every now and then in the coming weeks. Internalize it and focus your energy on being what you believe instead of what you look.

Set Goals and Develop an Action Plan

It is never too late to be what you might have been.

—GEORGE ELIOT

Find your vision or dream.

Have you ever had a dream or a vision where you saw yourself in a different place and time doing something you've always wanted to do?

> Walking across a stage in cap and gown to get your college diploma . . .
> Standing in a meadow miles away from roads and civilization . . .
> Cutting the ribbon at the grand opening of your own business . . .

What roadblocks have you created to keep you from getting there?

At the same instant you had the vision, did you automatically start coming up with a mental list of reasons you could not achieve that particular dream?

> Going back to college at my age is impractical.
> It costs too much money.
> I need the security of the job I have now.
> My husband wouldn't like it.

> What do I know about back-country hiking?
> I'm not in good enough shape.
> We don't have the money for all the equipment.
> Who would take care of the kids?

145

Women in pursuit of thinness often leave their other dreams behind. They talk themselves out of pursuing dreams because their creative vision and energy have already been stretched "too thin." Once we accept that being thin will not give us what we want out of life—that it is *not* the answer to life's troubles—we can focus on our other visions. We can choose to spend our creative, intuitive energies working toward goals that will get us where we want to be.

For the majority of women I've worked with, the hardest thing they will ever have to decide is what they *really* want to do with their life once they decide to stop dieting and abusing their body. It's such a difficult task because it often speaks to the core of what they are as a person, radically shifting their focus from what might have been or could be to the future and what *will* be, now that they have the energy to pursue their goals.

Yet, just as no one else is able to tell you what your values are or what you should weigh, you are the only person who can decide what your future will look like. You are the creator of your own destiny. If you don't draw your own road map, you will end up on someone else's detour.

Think back to how many times in your life you've stopped to realize that the task you're involved in, the work you're doing, or the pursuit you're following has been someone else's vision or goal. This can happen to us on a grand level, such as pursuing the college degree that our parents always expected was best for us or taking the job that didn't offer us growth but surely paid the bills.

But often this happens on a daily level as well, eroding our sense of direction and purpose for the goals *we* want to pursue. How much time do you spend on the phone each day with people who fritter away your valuable time? How often do you get sidetracked from your purpose by others' needs that seemingly outweigh your own?

Write down a few examples of times you have been distracted, on either a large or small scale, from your goals and purpose in life:

_____

_____

_____

_____

Often, dieting can undermine your self-confidence and perhaps cause you to unconsciously sabotage your greater life goals. "I'm too fat to ever get the job" or "He'll never ask me out because of my weight anyway" serve to distance us from our life purpose. By expecting the worst to happen and blaming your weight for problems, you may unknowingly set yourself up for failure before you even begin to pursue your goals. This attitude guarantees that things will go wrong and reinforces the "See, I told you so" belief. I call these habits stinkin' thinkin', and they can get in the way of living a happy, productive life as well.

Is there a dream or dreams you've left behind?

_____

_____

_____

_____

As you prepare to set your own goals, one helpful exercise is to think of one woman you respect immensely. She doesn't need to be someone you know personally. She might be a neighbor, a friend, a relative, someone connected to your profession, or a person you've read about.

Who do you look up to?

What traits does she have that you respect? What is it about her that you appreciate or enjoy? Try to describe her.

_____

_____

_____

_____

_____

_____

_____

As women, we don't have an "old-boy network."

One reason this can be helpful is that, as women, we don't have an "old-boy network." We aren't nearly as likely as men to have mentors—older friends or bosses who invest in our professional development and give us a model to follow as we strive for our goals.

The importance of role models is routinely stressed as extremely important for children and teens, but role models are equally important for women trying to carve a new path for their lives to follow— personally as well as professionally.

When we see other women accomplishing the type of things we care about, it is easier for us to convert our list of reasons we can't do something into a positive list of ways to accomplish our goals. Many women complain that they're too busy planning each day to take time to try to plan their lives, but we have to set goals before we can start creating our own maps.

Begin by projecting twenty years into the future. What would you like your life to look like then? Will you be at the height of your earning power? Thinking about retirement? Building a log cabin in the woods? Attending your children's college graduations? Attending your own graduation? I know twenty years is a long time ahead, but try to visualize at least a few pieces of that distant future.

In the space below, sketch an outline with words of the vision you have of yourself twenty years from now.

_____

_____

_____

_____

_____

Create a new vision.

Now come back to the present. To build a future, you have to start where you are right now. Do a little brainstorming in each of the following areas of your life, allowing whatever comes into your mind to go down on paper. As you go, keep in mind that your goal is to build a better future for yourself.

A relationship I would like to improve—how might I go about it?

_____

_____

_____

_____

My family life—how could it be better?

_____

_____

_____

_____

My time—could I manage it more wisely?

_____

_____

_____

_____

My social life—what could I do to find it more satisfying?

_____

_____

_____

_____

My job/profession—where do I want to go? What do I want to be?

_____

_____

_____

_____

Using that information, together with your philosophy statement and the information you have learned about yourself from other exercises, try to imagine what you would like your life to look like in one year. Try to form a visual picture of your whole life: your relationships, your profession, your character, your body, and all the other aspects of your whole being.

One year from now, how will my life be better? What will have changed?

_____

_____

_____

_____

Where will you be a year from now?

How will I be different? What new patterns of behavior will I be using? (Remember, you can consider only *your* behavior and not others'.)

_____

_____

_____

_____

What patterns of behavior will I have eliminated or lessened?

_____

_____

_____

_____

What are some of the things I will have accomplished?

_____

_____

_____

_____

Without a vision of the future, how can you create a map to get there?

What will be somewhat better than it is now? What will be remarkably better?

_____

_____

_____

_____

Who do I know that could be a model for me? Who is currently doing or accomplishing what I would like to do or accomplish?

_____

_____

_____

_____

How realistic is my vision? Can I accomplish it in one year?

_____

_____

_____

_____

Read through everything you wrote in this section. Give special consideration to achieving balance in your life. Do you need goals for your body, mind, and soul?

List three of your top goals for your future:

1. _____

2. _____

3. _____

One of the most common difficulties in goal setting is that we tend to make our goals too ambiguous. I am often amused by this goal: "I will watch what I eat." For some reason, I always envision those clients putting on their glasses and paying close attention to the pails of ice cream they're eating!

In addition to watching for ambiguity, you should make sure your goals meet these criteria:

Clearly defined goals are always specific . . .

- Each goal must be an accomplishment, achievement, or outcome.
- Each goal must be clear and specific.
- Each goal must be measurable.
- Each goal must be in keeping with your values.
- Each goal must be realistic, within your own control and your resources.
- Each goal must be able to be accomplished within a reasonable time frame. (*Not* I want a billion dollars in my savings account in five years.)

Here is an example of a goal that adheres to all the guidelines: "By the end of the year, I will have completed one computer course at the technical school in order to improve my computer skills." This goal clearly defines the who, what, where, and when.

Instead of saying, "I want to start an exercise program," you might want to put it this way: "I will start walking six blocks each morning at six-thirty, beginning on Monday. I will increase my walk by three blocks each week until I am walking twenty-four total blocks."

Instead of writing, "I want a new job," be more specific: "By Christmas, I will have found new work in an area that I enjoy."

Because these goals are more specific and measurable, they will be easier to attain. Look back at your goals. Do you need to restate them?

1. _____

2. _____

3. _____

You should now take a few minutes to consider how committed you are to these goals. Your level of commitment will play a big part in determining how successfully you can achieve them. Using the goals you just restated, ask yourself these questions about each one:

Make a commitment to seeing your goals become your future reality.

Am I choosing this goal freely?

1. _____
2. _____
3. _____

Is this goal one of a number of possibilities?

1. _____
2. _____
3. _____

Does this goal really appeal to me? Why or why not?

1. _____
2. _____
3. _____

What was the main reason I set this goal?

1. _____
2. _____
3. _____

How strong are my other reasons for setting it?

1. _____
2. _____
3. _____

Am I doing this for me or for someone else?

1. _____
2. _____
3. _____

Is the cost of pursuing this goal worth the benefits?

1. _____
2. _____
3. _____

Be open to opportunities. You may unexpectedly find the pot of gold at the end of a rainbow you almost missed!

Before you begin developing the action plans that will help you work out what steps you must take to achieve your goals, I encourage you to take a few moments to consider a concept that, in some lives, can be just as important as having goals: learning to recognize and take advantage of opportunities.

Often in life, we are given opportunities to do or accomplish something we never thought about before—something that never made it onto our list of goals because it was not in our current realm of realistic possibilities. In the military community, I often meet truly extraordinary women who cannot set any long-term goals relating to place because of the constant orders to move someplace else. Where others might complain or assign blame, many of these women become opportunists in the best sense of the word.

One of the happiest, most successful women I know moved twenty-one times in the twenty-seven years her husband served in the army. Because she saw each new place as an opportunity to experience something new, she was able to continue growing and learning while she worked in many different careers. Sometimes, she took a year or two off from any profession to reconnect with her children. During one of those off years, she started writing stories. Magazines bought them. Ultimately, she became a full-time writer who worked at home—wherever that happened to be—with a long list of corporate clients from earlier jobs and contacts. Twenty years ago, before computers and faxes and modems, she could not have envisioned such a career because it didn't exist. When the technology became available, she saw an opportunity and took it.

What opportunities occurred during the last year that took you by surprise? Did you take advantage of these opportunities, or did you let them pass by?

_____

_____

_____

_____

_____

_____

As you work on achieving your goals, keep the idea of opportunities in the back of your mind. You want to be flexible enough to recognize and take advantage of whatever special ones come your way.

Make an Action Plan for Life

If you think you can, you can. And if you think you can't, you're right.

—MARY KAY ASH

We are the hero of our own story.

—MARY MCCARTHY

Your action plans must fit you.

The final step on your journey to loving the body you were born with is to start realizing your hopes and dreams—to achieve your goals. No matter how wonderfully worded and well thought out your goals are, you need an action plan to make them happen. In reality, this is the most important part of each goal, because it lets you see clearly what steps you must take to get what you want.

For some of you, the action plans might be difficult to develop. They involve the use of unrestricted thinking and brainstorming—two concepts that you may not have practiced much in recent years. Don't let that deter you. Unrestricted thinking and brainstorming are just terms for putting your creative energies to good use. As you develop your action plans, write down every idea that pops into your head, no matter how wild or unrelated it may seem. By letting your mind have free rein, your creative energies can help you look at old problems in new ways.

Once you've removed everything connected with dieting from your "To Do" lists for each day, your action plans can fill the holes left in your calendar. Just remember that your action plans must fit *you*. They must be as specific as possible. If your goal is to start an exercise program, for example, your brainstorming session must address each detail that could sabotage or advance your goal.

Use your creative energies to brainstorm.

Start by deciding what types of exercise you truly enjoy. If you run into difficulty, think back to your childhood. Did you love to swim? Ride your bike? Roller skate? Once you know what you like to do, think about what kinds of equipment you might need. Do you need to watch for a sale on walking shoes? Do you need to save money for the sale? What will you do if the weather is bad? What other activity might you substitute?

Now think of more questions that need to be answered:

Who will watch the children?
Can they come along?
Are there friends who may enjoy going with me?
Will the dinner hour need to change so I can get out and do it?
Might breakfast time work better? Very early in the morning?
What about sore muscles?
Do I need to allow time to stretch—soak in the tub?

In my own case, I love to exercise in the morning, before my days get too busy. Because the light changes with each season, I have to allow for these changes in my daily plans. During the winter, I need to walk in areas with sufficient light, closer to home. During the summer, I can wander farther afield, exploring new areas in the early sunrise light.

Each detail you can anticipate will move you closer to achieving success.

Following is an example of what an action plan might look like for the one goal I know you will probably have: loving the body you were born with! As you look at the sample action plan, keep in mind that yours will look different. Each action plan is unique to the individual. To be successful, yours should include the things that you *want* to do, *can* do, and would *love* to do if you just gave yourself permission to do them.

SAMPLE GOAL AND ACTION PLAN

Goal:

I will learn to love the body I was born with and to appreciate all the gifts that make me who I am as an individual.

*How to translate
your goals into
actions.*

Action Plan:

I will say one positive thing to myself every time I stand in front of a
mirror.

I will enroll in the yoga class that starts next month at the
YWCA.

I will add new spices and flavorings to my food.

This year I will make one Christmas gift by hand, for Aunt Agatha,
so that I can renew my creative energies.

I will speak loudly against dieting when any of my girlfriends brings
up the subject.

I will recognize my multiple roles and set boundaries on my time by
clearly stating my limits to the people in my life.

I will spend twenty minutes every Monday afternoon after work
walking through the woods.

I will discuss with my partner all of the negative things I feel about
my body during sex.

I will buy new potpourri for the house and put it in the rooms where
I spend the most time.

I will tear through the house and throw out every diet book, diet
food, and exercise gizmo I have wasted my money on.

I will try not to eat portions larger than the size of my fist.

I will start every day by singing at least one song while I'm taking
my morning shower.

I have used goals and action plans since I was a young girl, when my
father would constantly pester me about *what* I wanted to do and then
how I meant to do it. I would often get so fed up with his persistence I
wanted to scream, but the lessons I learned early have proven to be
fruitful as an adult.

My dream had always been to visit France. I had studied French in
school for eight years, and I wanted to go there and learn more about
the culture. But I wasn't anywhere near able to just jump off the couch
and book a flight! I had to put an action plan into place in order to
make it work. This plan is another example of creating an action plan
from a goal.

Goal:

In the summer of 1993, my husband and I will travel through France on bicycles for two weeks.

Seems like a pretty simple goal, right? But look at the action plan it took to make it happen.

Action Plan:

One year ahead:

Call travel agent and determine approximate costs for travel and lodging.

Divide costs into fifty-two weeks to determine the sum of money that must be saved each week.

Decide what is unessential and can be eliminated in the weekly budget.

Go to the bank and open a savings account separate from others.

Go to library and check out books of possible regions in France amenable to bike riding.

Talk to friends who have traveled to France to gain their experience and knowledge.

Six months ahead:

Begin watching for sales on backpacking tents and pannier bags for bike.

Start vigorous exercise program to include biking fifty total miles per week, plus other activities.

Hire a trainer at the gym to teach me strength training suitable for extended bike riding.

Check out audiotapes at library to begin refreshing my French while driving in the car.

Begin investigating possible sources of child care for two weeks.

One month ahead:

Pay visit to travel agent and purchase tickets. Make final lodging arrangements.

Purchase any final equipment needed for trip.
Confirm child care arrangements.
Visit lawyer to update will and custodial arrangements.

One week ahead:

Pack equipment and gear on bikes for final practice ride.
Read up on assistance in preventing physical effects of time changes.
Ensure all children's needs are provided for in our absence.
Practice, practice, practice reading and writing French.

Each step in the action plan played an important part in achieving the end goal. Many people pass through life always wishing for what might have been or could have been. Without an action plan, there is no way to bring these dreams to fulfillment, and before you know it, years have passed without the dreams ever coming true.

The lists could go on and on, but these two action plans should give you the idea. Now it's your turn! Go back to the goals you wrote earlier. Write three separate goals at the top of three pieces of paper. Let your creative forces go, and develop your own action plans.

As you developed your action plans, you may have noticed that you needed help in some places to realize your goals. Now is a good time to think about the people and resources you have available.

What resources do you need?

Who can help you achieve your goals? What people in your life will be resources for you?

_____

_____

_____

What resources, both inside and outside of you, can you use?

_____

_____

_____

What places might you need to be in order to accomplish your goals?

_____

_____

How does time work for you? against you?

_____

_____

What forces will move you forward? hold you back?

List the forces that will support you in pursuit of your goals. For example, "I am a self-motivated person" or "The good feeling of having control of my life again."

_____

_____

_____

List the forces that might restrain you: "I have a difficult time getting up off the couch" or "I've tried shooting for my dreams before and it never worked" (*stinkin' thinkin'*).

_____

_____

_____

Set priorities within each action plan.

Look through each of your action plans one more time. Decide which actions are the most important for helping you realize that particular goal. Prioritize each action in your plan by assigning numbers: #1, #2, #3 . . .

Now try to visualize how other people are likely to feel about your goals. For example, if one of your goals is to love your body the way it is, how might your friends react when you start speaking up about the futility and danger of dieting? How might your partner feel and react when you begin to feel proud of the body you live in?

_____

_____

_____

_____

_____

None of your goals will be achieved if you do not take the important step of transposing your action plans to your "To Do" lists for today and tomorrow and each day after that. Post your three primary goals someplace where you will see them often—you want them integrated into your life. Tape them to your bathroom mirror. Post them on the refrigerator. Stick them to the sun visor in your car. These actions will also help affirm for others in your life the direction you are choosing to take.

Your new road map will give you power over your own life . . .

As you begin to implement your life's goals, interesting things will begin to happen. The focus in your life will change from degrading and abusing your body to using your body as a friend to help you achieve your goals. You will feel more powerful. You will control your own destiny. You will be able to bypass the external demands that our culture has been placing on you.

. . . and help you empower others!

This is exactly why the diet industry and our male-dominated social system perpetuate the myth that thinness = attractiveness = happiness. If we are off-centered, hungry, and apathetic, we are more likely to play by their rules instead of asserting our own power and purposes. Feeding and caring for your body while living a well-balanced life will make you strong enough to stand up and scream at the inequities of our current system. You will be strong enough to choose not to accept someone else's idea of beauty. Perhaps you will even be strong enough to get angry, speak out, create political agendas, and empower your sisters and daughters and mothers to do the same!

How We Can *All* Love the Bodies We Were Born With

Someday perhaps change will occur when times are ready for it instead of always when it is too late. Someday change will be accepted as life itself.

—SHIRLEY MACLAINE

Is it possible to believe all women could love their bodies?

None of us chose the body we inhabit. We were all born with certain physical characteristics we had no control over. Our basic body sizes and shapes, like the color of our eyes, hair, and skin, were all genetically predetermined. In this melting pot of a country, where our physical characteristics are as varied as our ethnic, religious, and historical heritages, isn't it reasonable to assume we should all be encouraged to love and accept who and what we are?

Because the worship of thinness has become so commonplace in America that it crosses all social and ethnic lines, at first glance it may seem impossible to change society to the point where all women could begin to love the bodies they were born with. Look closer and it does not seem like such an impossible dream at all.

Anything is possible when we work together.

While the diet, fashion, and advertising industries would surely put up a fight, just imagine what could happen if the entire community of health professionals joined forces with the millions of women who are fed up with an unattainable, unhealthy cultural "ideal." Working

162

together, how long would it take to debunk the myth that thinness equals happiness?

We could quite possibly eradicate the devastating effects of anorexia nervosa, bulimia, and semistarvation diets in one generation. Consider that twenty years ago no one would have believed that smoking would have become such a social stigma in our culture, and you can envision the potential for change. We could greatly reduce the serious medical consequences of yo-yo dieting and compulsive overeating. We could increase our country's productivity tenfold as our hungry, size-obsessed population turned their attention to more fruitful endeavors.

Where would we begin? At home, of course, with reinforcement from community and family education programs at the grassroots level that stress good eating habits and sensitivity to body image at every level of development.

INFANCY

Infancy provides the foundations for the feeding relationship between parents and children. Infancy is characterized by rapid physical growth. Parents with their own feeding agendas for the infant can alter the child's eating habits early on. Following your health care provider's guidelines for the healthiest milk feeding, the introduction of solid foods, and introducing liquids from a cup can be beneficial in establishing early on a healthy feeding relationship.

- Teach parents to be attentive to their baby's cues of satiety and trust her natural appetite so they can recognize when she has had enough.
- Discourage the "just a little bit more" feeding syndrome.
- Stress that touching and cuddling by both parents are more important than extra food for fostering the healthy growth and development of infants.

TODDLERHOOD (AGES TWO TO FOUR)

By the age of two, the rapid physical growth begins to slow dramatically, and consequently, so does the child's appetite. If the child continued to grow at the same level it did during infancy, you'd have a five-year-old the size of an elephant! Many parents see this as a problem and attempt to override the child's natural appetites. (Have you ever seen a parent trying to "fly" into a toddler's mouth with a spoonful of food?) Physically, children at this stage are elongating and building muscle tissue through the use of their body, as well as building important bone strength.

The environment around them is the priority for toddlers, and their new-found freedom to walk and run gives them the vehicle to explore their world. Toddlers will begin to assert their independence and use food as one of the few things they have any control over. They are strongly influenced by media and their peers and will imitate behaviors they see their parents do.

Each stage of life plays a role in developing a healthy body image.

- Emphasize that messy self-feeding is a necessary part of healthy development.
- Help parents accept the cues of hunger and satiety that toddlers display, and stress the importance of not forcing or withholding food from them.
- Encourage parents to offer a wide range of healthy food choices, allowing the child to choose the portion. Parents should also accept the toddler's readiness to hold a spoon and a cup and not resent the loss of bottle or breast feeding.
- Instead of food rewards, use hugs!

EARLY CHILDHOOD (AGES FOUR TO NINE)

Though still a period of physical growth for the child, the priority will be on intellectual development. This is an age of increased ability to develop social relationships and an expanding world beyond the family with the start of school. These children will mimic the attitudes of their friends, family, and what they see on television.

This is a time of academic and athletic competition. Feelings of inferiority may arise, including the fear of not meeting adult expectations academically or socially. Hero worship persists, especially of rock stars, athletes and coaches, and teachers. Prejudice and self-concern about obesity begins.

- You are still their hero! They will mimic your food choices.
- While basic limitations on eating behavior need to be established, young children should not be forced to have perfect etiquette, but teach that there are rules to be obeyed at the table.
- Offer plenty of healthy snacks.
- To prevent later problems, parents should not allow power struggles over food, never lecture about wasted food, and never refer to dieting.
- Young children should become involved in their parents' active lifestyle and learn fun ways of being fit.
- Instead of food rewards, continue using hugs! Each hug a child receives reinforces her self-esteem and worthiness in this world. Always be nurturing her positive feelings about the body she was born with.
- Discuss children's early questions about the body and sexuality with honesty and respect.
- Introduce children to a broad range of new foods and flavors, but don't force them to try them. Present new foods frequently, and most children will eventually try—and like—most of them.
- Parents need to control the grocery budget and not be influenced by the child's susceptibility to commercials. Limiting television viewing helps.
- Involve children in the food purchasing and preparation processes. Allow them to practice their reading and decision-making skills on food labels at the supermarket.

LATE CHILDHOOD (AGES TEN TO THIRTEEN)

Girls will have a growth spurt to approximately 98 percent of adult height, and sexual development, including menstruation, may begin. Boys' physical growth is latent.

This age is often accompanied by fads in dress, foods, and activities. Children may feel conflicts between their needs for independence and security. Body image may become distorted and frequently is demonstrated by negative thoughts about oneself. Alcohol or drug use may begin.

- Continue to engage children in the family's recreational and fitness activities. Also encourage activities that increase self-esteem and help children feel productive.
- Do not mention the child's changing body size.
- Discuss sexuality as a normal part of life.
- Your openness and willingness to discuss her fears about her changing body will encourage positive feelings and esteem in young women this age.

ADOLESCENCE (AGES FOURTEEN TO SEVENTEEN)

Girls' growth rate slows. Girls find they need fewer calories to maintain their weight compared to just a short time ago. Girls have gained an average of 10 percent body fat over the last few years, while boys will have lost an average of 5 percent. Boys will experience a huge growth spurt, and their sexual development begins.

Peer pressure becomes enormous. Adolescents separate from parental authority. They search for their individual identity. Weight becomes a significant issue, both personally and socially. Those not of ideal weight are not considered the "in" group. Sexual experimentation usually begins or continues.

- Offer adolescents a wide range of foods, including bountiful snacks to compensate for their growing bodies.
- Promote health and function of their bodies instead of size and shape.
- Encourage adolescents to be responsible for their own nutritional status.
- Communicate openly on issues concerning sexuality, but do not make negative mention of pubertal changes. Help adolescents accept themselves as they are and promote activities that enhance self-esteem.
- If media/peer influences on body size become a factor, continue to stress the importance of self-acceptance and healthy eating habits as well as the wonders of diversity.
- Engage adolescents in creative endeavors that allow them to feel

purposeful and productive. Focus on their skills rather than their appearance.

- Discuss natural sexual desires with young women, as well as their consequences and alternative forms of expression.

EARLY ADULTHOOD (AGES EIGHTEEN TO TWENTY-FIVE)

Assuming the adolescent has successfully achieved a healthy self-identity, this stage is characterized by the search for intimacy. Intimacy need not involve sexuality exclusively but also relationships between friends. Intimacy here means the ability to share with and care about another person without fear of losing oneself in the process. Young adults with negative self-worth and body image will have difficulty achieving intimacy in relationships with others and may feel isolated and alone.

- While some dissatisfaction with body size and shape may be inevitable, young adults should be encouraged to focus on education, career, and personal goals instead of their bodies.
- Both men and women should discuss the "perfection expectation" common to this age group—and its negative consequences on full, rich, reciprocal relationships.

ADULTHOOD

We control our vision of our future.

By adulthood, the person begins to be concerned with others beyond his immediate family—with future generations, and the nature of the society and the world in which those generations will live. This is not exclusively the concern of those who are parents but can be found in any individual who actively concerns herself with the welfare of young people and with making the world a better place for them to live and work in. Those adults who have successfully navigated through earlier stages with a strong sense of self and identity will see their bodies as healthy vehicles to help them pursue their life purpose. Adults who appreciate the vast differences between different types of bodies might display attitudes and life-style behaviors similar to these:

- Enjoyable exercise is a daily part of life.
- Meals consist of quickly prepared foods with rich, profound flavors.
- Diets and their accompanying clubs, aids, and foods are not an accepted part of life.
- Nonfood rewards provide respite from the pressures of raising a family and starting a career.
- The disastrous effects of losing and gaining weight are common knowledge—these women refuse to ride the diet roller coaster.
- Males appreciate the changing bodies that represent a woman's life cycle.
- Bowing to public pressure, the media now includes realistic images of women and men of all ages and sizes.

Our children deserve a healthy legacy for their future. Let's give it to them.

The time has come . . .

. . . to challenge the cultural values and ideals of our society.

. . . for health professionals to become leaders in fostering a rational, healthy, humane approach to body size.

. . . for us to learn to love our own bodies and define our identity in broad terms incorporating all that we are as women.

. . . to believe once and for all that dieting does not work.

. . . to preach loudly against the worship of thinness.

. . . to teach our young that a thinner body is *not* an answer to anything at all.

We must refuse to participate in cultural stereotypes:

- Eliminate all of our negative language, especially about the obese.
- Speak loudly about the dangers of repeated dieting.

continued

- Expand the standard of feminine beauty to include a celebration of all that is feminine.
- Teach our sons that women are not ornaments, so they can appreciate them for all of their qualities and in all of their sizes.
- Teach our daughters to be rich, balanced women who *love, respect,* and *value* their bodies.

As women who have finally learned to love the bodies we were born with, let us revel in:

- the thrill our future holds
- the creativity that nurtures our lives
- our wisdom to know what is best for our own bodies, and
- our strength to seek change for the future!

Additional Reading

Anderson, S. & Hopkins, P. *The Feminist Face of God: The Unfolding of the Sacred in Women.* New York: Bantam, 1991.

Bordo, S. *Unbearable Weight: Feminism, Western Culture, and the Body.* Berkeley: University of California Press, 1993.

Brumberg, J. *Fasting Girls.* Cambridge: Harvard University Press, 1988.

Freedman, R. *Bodylove: Learning to Like Our Looks and Ourselves.* New York: Harper & Row, 1988.

Green, J. *Food for Love: Healing the Food, Sex, Love and Intimacy Relationship.* New York: Pocket Books, 1993.

Orbach, S. *Fat Is a Feminist Issue.* New York: Berkley Books, 1978.

Pinkola-Estes, C. *Women Who Run With the Wolves: Myths and Stories of the Female Archetype.* New York: Ballantine Books, 1993.

Rodin, J. *Body Traps.* New York: William Morrow, 1992.

Weiss, L. & Meadow, R. *Women's Conflicts About Eating and Sexuality: The Relationship Between Food and Sex.* New York: Harper & Row, 1992.

Wolf, N. *The Beauty Myth.* New York: Harper and Row, 1991.

About the Author

MONICA DIXON, M.S., R.D., designs and delivers seminars, facilitates retreats and presents motivational keynote addresses at conventions and business meetings across the country. A former university instructor, health counselor, and hospital outpatient dietitian, Monica has worked extensively with women of all ages and walks of life in both the public and private sectors, helping them empower their lives through the use of inner and outer resources.

She has a master's degree in Counselor Education, a bachelor's degree in Dietetics, and is currently completing her doctoral work in health psychology, where she is researching the complex psychological factors involved when individuals make lifestyle choices.

Monica speaks to thousands of people of varied backgrounds each year on a wide range of issues, including communication and counseling in the health sciences, motivating individuals toward healthy lifestyles, and the role of food and body image in women's sexuality.

DIAGNOSIS AT YOUR FINGERTIPS—
FROM H. WINTER GRIFFITH, M.D.,
ONE OF AMERICA'S MOST TRUSTED FAMILY PHYSICIANS

__COMPLETE GUIDE TO PEDIATRIC SYMPTOMS, ILLNESS & MEDICATIONS   0-895-86816-4/$14.95
The most complete guide to treating sick children from infancy through adolescence arranged in quick reference health sections. Includes thousands of symptoms and medications.

__COMPLETE GUIDE TO PRESCRIPTION & NONPRESCRIPTION DRUGS, 1996   0-399-52161-5/$15.95
The thirteenth edition of this bestselling reference book.
"Comprehensive, easy-to-use, and informative."—*Los Angeles Times*

__COMPLETE GUIDE TO PRESCRIPTION AND NONPRESCRIPTION PEDIATRIC DRUGS by H. Winter Griffith, M.D. and Victor A. Elsberry, Pharm.D. *(Coming April 1996)*   0-399-51994-7/$15.95
Specifically for children from infancy through twelve years old, this reference guide gives important information for over 300 pediatric drugs.

__COMPLETE GUIDE TO SPORTS INJURIES 0-399-51712-X/$15.95
Dr. Griffith shows how to recognize and treat hundreds of the most common sports injuries. Highly recommended for all coaches, parents, and athletes.

__COMPLETE GUIDE TO SYMPTOMS, ILLNESS & SURGERY (3rd Edition)   0-399-51942-4/$15.95
Helps you diagnose, understand, and seek treatment for any illness, from the common cold to life-threatening cancer or heart disease.

__COMPLETE GUIDE TO SYMPTOMS, ILLNESS & SURGERY FOR PEOPLE OVER 50   0-399-51749-9/$19.00
The most comprehensive medical reference for older Americans, featuring hundreds of symptoms and what they mean with suggestions for treatment.